Preaching without Borders

Preaching without Borders

The Challenges and Blessings of Expository
Preaching in a Multi-Ethnic Church

Ryan Roach

Foreword by Steven D. Mathewson

WIPF & STOCK · Eugene, Oregon

PREACHING WITHOUT BORDERS
The Challenges and Blessings of Expository Preaching in a Multi-Ethnic Church

Copyright © 2022 Ryan Roach. All rights reserved. Except for brief quotations in critical publications or reviews, no part of this book may be reproduced in any manner without prior written permission from the publisher. Write: Permissions, Wipf and Stock Publishers, 199 W. 8th Ave., Suite 3, Eugene, OR 97401.

Wipf & Stock
An Imprint of Wipf and Stock Publishers
199 W. 8th Ave., Suite 3
Eugene, OR 97401

www.wipfandstock.com

PAPERBACK ISBN: 978-1-6667-3832-2
HARDCOVER ISBN: 978-1-6667-9886-9
EBOOK ISBN: 978-1-6667-9887-6

09/02/22

To Morgan,
who has given me great
freedom to pursue my passion.

Contents

Foreword | ix
Acknowledgements | xi

1　The Need for Cross-Ethnic Preaching | 1
2　Building a Cross-Ethnic Ministerial Philosophy | 13
3　Intercultural Communication at Work | 24
4　How the Gospel Changes Everything | 38
5　How Does Expository Preaching Fit in a Multi-Ethnic Church? | 57
6　Possibilities of Preaching to a Multi-Ethnic Church | 83
7　What Happens If We Do Not Adapt? | 100
8　What Preachers Can Do | 114

Bibliography | 131

Foreword

HADDON ROBINSON USED TO say that good expository preaching is not simply talking to people about the Bible. Rather, it is talking to people from the Bible about themselves. This requires us to understand the people to whom we preach.

The first two churches where I served as a pastor were in Montana. One was in Helena, the state capitol, and the other was near Bozeman— a university community. I loved the diversity in those congregations and the challenge of preaching to people with various social, economic, and vocational backgrounds. We had blue-collar folks, white-collar folks, and ranchers. We had fourth generation Montanans and new residents from places like Seattle and the Silicon Valley. We had church members who lived in mobile homes and others who lived in large houses with stunning mountain views. This required preaching in a way that related to the diverse perspectives and needs of these congregations.

But there was little ethnic diversity. We had a handful of Montana State University students from Asia or India. Yet most in our congregation were Caucasian and of European descent.

Then I accepted the call to pastor a church in the north suburbs of Chicago. The ethnic diversity of the church was significant. The first month I was there, I noticed that we had people who had moved to the Chicago area from South Africa, England, Kenya, Nigeria, Chile, and India. Suddenly,

Foreword

I had to make adjustments to the way I preached. It was not simply the illustrations I used or the cultural references I included in my preaching. I had to adjust to different ways of thinking.

Western culture is typically individualistic and thinks about the gospel of Jesus Christ in terms of guilt and innocence. However, I discovered that some in our congregation were from shame-honor cultures. They placed greater emphasis on the expectations of the community and thus thought in terms of how the gospel restores a person's honor and removes their shame. A few African families came from animistic contexts in which fear of evil led people to pursue power over the spirit world. This framework let them to see the gospel in terms of Christ's power over the forces of evil.

It took me awhile to adjust to this multi-ethnic context, and I'm still learning fifteen years later!

This is why I am thankful for Ryan Roach's work on this challenge. Dr. Roach writes as a veteran pastor who is committed to expository preaching and has done it in multi-ethnic, multi-racial contexts. He loves the truth that Christ, with his blood, has "purchased for God persons from every tribe and language and people and nation" (Rev 5:9). It's a glorious vision, but one that makes the task of preaching even more complex.

How can a preacher "preach without borders" to a local congregation that has people from diverse ethnic backgrounds? This book will guide you. Take it and read. Then use its insights as you preach to the diverse group of people in your local church—people that God has redeemed from a multiplex of racial and ethnic backgrounds.

Steven D. Mathewson
Director of the Doctor of Ministry program
Western Seminary, Portland, Oregon

Acknowledgements

THE PEOPLE WHO BELONG here first are the ones who share a home with me. My wife Morgan has been calm and steady during our marriage, allowing me to be outside of the house strange hours serving the church. My kids have understood the same thing and have always given me grace. My parents have also been instrumental in getting me to this point, most notably the twenty-plus years I spent living in their home and occasionally causing mischief.

Though I have been a pastor at four churches and a member at a few more, Pursuit Church in Orlando, FL, was the place where I learned to preach and found a passion for multi-ethnic ministry. This project would have never been started without the faithfulness and encouragement of the elders and members there.

First Baptist Church Alcoa not only gave me a chance to pastor but also the freedom to continue in this effort. Many of the members provided sustained encouragement that pushed me to the finish line.

My time as a student at Western Seminary had some difficulties but a few faculty members stand out: Dr. Steve Mathewson, Dr. Reid Kisling, Dr. John Kwak, and Dr. John Branner all read through my work and provided feedback that I desperately needed to hear.

Many pastors have helped me along the journey in both ministry and in my research. Bill Barnett, Brian Watson, Clint Goode, Justin Benson,

Acknowledgements

Mark Lauterbach, and Nathan Kollar listened to me complain and always sought to give sound guidance and encouragement. These men are the best examples of what a faithful shepherd should be.

Pastors often struggle to maintain friendships with members of their church, and I am no different. The few best friends that I have had mean the world to me. Bob Sweeney was a rock when I was at the worst point in my life. I wanted to leave ministry many times and he always pulled me back to reality. Emi Romero and Bryan Rosenbaum are two of my best friends. They allowed me to be myself and were not afraid to tell me when I was being stupid. Bob, Emi, and Bryan taught me that I needed friends more than a platform.

1

The Need for Cross-Ethnic Preaching

THE FIRST CHURCH I pastored was a strange place and I would not have had it any other way. Though I have been called to serve in a new setting, I miss my strange church family. By strange, I do not mean that it is heretical or heterodox in any way. Quite the contrary, my church was a strange place because we were ethnically diverse, which was an entirely new experience for me, as every church I had ever served in or attended consisted of a white majority. These were excellent churches with faithful pastors and Christians who deeply loved the Lord, but they were not integrated. They did not look like the neighborhoods and communities which surrounded the church property.

But my church was different. We resembled the community of the city of Orlando (and our neighborhood) quite well and that was clear from the moment one walked into the building. We had Malaysians, Ethiopians, Puerto Ricans, Kenyans, Colombians, Mexicans, Costa Ricans, Dominicans, Cubans, Uruguayans, Haitians, Japanese, Chinese, and even an Alaskan as part of our church during my pastorate.

My church was strange, with a membership makeup of only half Anglo. My prayer is that other churches will become like we were in representing their respective communities so that one day, having such a diverse congregation will not be so strange. The more time I spent in prayer, in my study, and in the pulpit, the more I got a slight glimpse of the beauty of heaven because I saw how the gospel goes beyond our differences and brings unity around the common goal of glorifying Christ. I want my fellow pastors to experience this as well.

My hope in this area is not simply to appear multi-cultural or to be well-liked because I follow a popular trend. My hope in preaching, pastoral ministry, and everything else I do is found in the hope of being made right with God through the perfect obedience and sacrificial death of Christ.[1] What is needed from preachers and pastors is more than making claims that diversity is admirable and excellent. We need more than progressive or politically correct messages. Our focus in ministry must be all about the gospel and how the message that we carry is the only way to bridge the racial and ethnic divides that infect our communities, schools, and congregations.

My hope is that none of us should ever want to put limits on the gospel. In the pages that follow, I hope to show how easy it can be, however, to overlook important issues of race, culture, and ethnicity in our preaching and, most importantly, how the gospel addresses those things. This mostly unintentional oversight to apply the gospel cracks open the chasm between the preacher and his listeners because it misses the application of the gospel to issues that matter to many. The gospel changed us at the moment of our conversion, and it is still changing us as we grow in holiness. That experience and life-altering truth should be the catalyst for us to remove any impediments that limit our effectiveness to proclaim the gospel of Jesus Christ from the pulpit every week.

The Modern Landscape

Though it certainly seems like racial tension and political discord are sending American churches down a path where homogeneity in the local church is the future, with further integration in America there will come a need for further integration of American churches. And if our churches are to be more integrated than they are now, our preaching must adapt as well. With joy we celebrate the church plants and revitalization efforts, but the movement must continue and the first step we can take as preachers is to be more mindful of our audience as well as the needs and burdens they carry.

This journey will not be easy, but it is desperately needed. For preachers of previous generations, the movement toward a diverse congregation is likely a new concept. Not long ago, most churches were segregated because

1. A more detailed view of the gospel is discussed in chapter 4.

most communities were segregated. Black churches in the United States were not formed due to voluntary segregation. Rather, black Christians were not allowed full membership at white churches so they were forced to start churches where they could serve and use their gifts.

A 2015 report by the United States Census Bureau states that by 2044, "more than half of all Americans are projected to belong to a minority group; and by 2060, nearly one in five of the nation's total population is projected to be foreign born."[2] Today's white population will soon be the minority, and in many cities this is already the case.[3] Some pastors may be tempted to brush this off and continue living and worshipping in their preferred way because it is easier and safer, but the gospel must change how we see those who are different because Christ has united his people as brothers and sisters. If we live with a focus on the gospel in our lives and ministry, we will be open to adapt and possibly even change our ministry methods (while staying biblical) in order to give the gospel to current and future generations.

Bryan Chappell, a pastor, former seminary president, and one of the foremost experts on expository preaching, recognizes how life (at least in the United States) has changed. He writes,

> A Hindu is someone I meet on the street, not a distant pagan . . . in Delhi. A Muslim is the respectful student that sits next to me in a university class, not a robed Saracen brandishing a crescent sword in a black and white movie starring Errol Flynn. Three to five million Buddhists live in the United States. Miami is now the unofficial capital of Latin America. Los Angeles and New York are home to literally hundreds of language groups. A quarter of the residents of California are foreign born.[4]

These discussions about our preaching and the church in the United States can be much more beneficial if we see our churches and our communities for what they are—a mission field. We no longer need to travel thousands of miles to share the gospel with someone who speaks a different language, comes from a different culture, or follows a different religious worldview. By living in a city or even a suburb, we quickly discover that

---

2. Colby and Ortman, "Projections of the Size and Composition of the U.S. Population: 2014 to 2060."

3. "Share of Population by Race/Ethnicity," *Heller School for Social Policy and Management at Brandeis University*.

4. Chappell, "Necessity of Preaching Christ," 62.

those we once travelled to share the gospel with are now our neighbors and co-workers.

Author and professor J.D. Payne notes that the church is to be on mission until Jesus returns because it is God who has brought the world to us. He explains, "While a major part of making disciples occurs as we go throughout the world (Matt 28:19), we must realize that the divine Maestro has been orchestrating the movement of peoples into our neighborhoods. He has been bringing the peoples of the uttermost parts of the world into our communities."[5]

Even with the changes in the demographic landscape, many American churches are lagging behind the rest of society in terms of integration. John Perkins, who has personally experienced the horrors of racism in the South, has written about this problem extensively. In his book, *Dream With Me: Race, Love, and the Struggle We Must Win*, he argues, "We claim to be an ethnic 'melting pot,' yet people of different nationalities and backgrounds—black, white, Latino, Asian, Eastern European—most often worship with people who look, act, and talk like themselves." He refers to Jesus' prayer in John 17 that Christians would have unity: "Yet, on Sunday morning, we seldom model this reality of the gospel."[6] Perkins echoes the famous statement made by Dr. Martin Luther King, Jr. on the American television show *Meet the Press* in April 1960: "I think it is one of the tragedies of our nation, one of the shameful tragedies, that eleven o'clock on Sunday morning is one of the most segregated hours, if not the most segregated hours, in Christian America."[7]

Even though Sunday mornings are often segregated hours, there is hope. Prolific scholar and researcher Michael Emerson observes, "In 1998 a national study of American congregations found that just 5 percent of Protestant churches were racially diverse (no one racial group is 80 percent or more of the congregation)." When the same study was conducted nine years later, the researchers found that large Protestant churches were three times more likely to be multiracial. That change took place in just nine years! The study found that in evangelical churches, large congregations were five times more likely to be multiracial.[8] This is great news, but most churches are not large and are more likely to remain dominated by a single ethnic or cultural makeup.

5. Payne, *Strangers Next Door,*, 22–23.
6. Perkins, *Dream With Me*, 45.
7. "Interview with Dr. Martin Luther King, Jr."
8. Emerson, *Leading a Healthy Multi-Ethnic Church*, 15.

The Need for Cross-Ethnic Preaching

Mark DeYmaz, a pastor and author who is well-known for his experience and research in the area of pastoring multi-ethnic congregations, takes an immensely optimistic view of the future makeup of the American church. He believes that by 2050, 50 percent of American churches will achieve 50 percent diversity.[9] This belief is based on the demographic cultural trends of integration in society and a strong hope that the church can make the necessary changes to advance the gospel to everyone, regardless of the barriers that have prevented it from moving in the past.

As followers of Christ, we have the solution for the problems that the world faces. Racism, ethnocentrism, and political battles over immigration and racial disparities are issues Christians can address from a gospel-centered perspective. In other words, the church is in a unique position to deal with problems that plague modern day culture. DeYoung, et al., write,

> The twenty-first century holds the potential to be the century of the multiracial congregation, despite the relatively small percentage such churches represent among total congregations. The broad population shifts taking place in the United States are expected by the midpoint of the century to produce a country with a racial demographic that is very diverse and without a numeric majority. Such changes produce settings with an increased possibility for multiracial congregations. A movement toward more multiracial congregations must be the cutting edge for ministry and growth in this century.[10]

This statement is echoed by Edward Gilbreath in his book *Reconciliation Blues: A Black Evangelical's Inside View of White Christianity*. As the title suggests, the author shares his understanding of how he (a black man) relates to American evangelicalism (largely white). He remarks that even though the church is certainly not perfect, it is the one institution equipped to deal with the racial divide. Gilbreath references the anti-slavery movement in the nineteenth century and the civil rights movement of the twentieth century as examples of how the church was at the center of the struggle for justice. He notes, "In both of these cases, the faithful response of a few daring believers gave way to powerful demonstrations of God's deliverance, justice and grace. After a long human struggle, God broke through."[11]

---

9. DeYmaz and Li, *Leading a Healthy Multi-Ethnic Church*, 28.
10. DeYoung et al., *United by Faith*, 74.
11. Gilbreath, *Reconciliation Blues*, 21.

This example of dealing with justice issues should give hope to everyone who has a desire to reach their neighbors with the gospel of reconciliation to God and, as part of the covenant of the gospel in our own lives, reconciliation to one another. Our focus in our preaching should not be to build a kingdom of our own, make a name for ourselves, become a famous conference speaker, or write books. Those are the world's values, but our value is not in how good we are or what we do. Instead, our value is found in what Christ has already done for us through his perfect life, sacrificial death, glorious resurrection, and coming triumphant return. The good news of Christ's achievement is what we are to give to our people every time we step behind the pulpit to open God's word, anything less being a dereliction of our duty.

Why This Study?

This study is needed and the reason is simple. My aim is to challenge preachers to think through their sermons, from the beginning of their preparation as they are pondering the scheduled text all the way to the conclusion of the message they deliver on Sunday morning. The lack of multi-ethnic awareness and application in sermons is certainly not done on purpose or from a heart that does not care about ethnic groups outside of the preacher's own groups. The problem is simply not thought of much. Little has been written on leading multi-ethnic churches and even less on preaching in a multi-ethnic setting. Scripture is not silent on ethnic diversity in the church. Chapter two of this study dives into some of the scriptural examples of tension between ethnic groups (Jews and Gentiles) in the early church.

Beyond that, I have been challenged in my own churches to preach in such a way that everyone will hear and understand the gospel presented and have an opportunity to respond. In Romans 10, Paul writes,

> For the Scripture says, "Everyone who believes in him will not be put to shame." For there is no distinction between Jew and Greek; for the same Lord is Lord of all, bestowing his riches on all who call on him. For "everyone who calls on the name of the Lord will be saved." How then will they call on him in whom they have not believed? And how are they to believe in him of whom they have never heard? And how are they to hear without someone preaching? (Romans 10:11–14 ESV)

The Need for Cross-Ethnic Preaching

It is clear from this passage that God has called every Christian to proclaim the gospel and preachers have an audience to hear it every week.

But there are often impediments that arise in our preaching. In the United States, there is an often-unspoken chasm which exists between black and white and, in the pulpit, most pastors unknowingly contribute to the divide. According to Emerson and Smith, two scholars who spent time examining the problem of race in America, the divide does not come from outright racism. Instead, what they call *racialization* "understands that racial practices that reproduce racial division . . . (1) are increasingly covert, (2) are embedded in normal operations of institutions, (3) avoid direct racial terminology, and (4) are invisible to most Whites."[12] The racial division Emerson and Smith discuss is not direct racism found with groups like the Ku Klux Klan.

We all have different preferences and activities we like and we all bring those into our church families. This is well-understood, but what is overlooked is how different those interests can be and what impact that has on the church body and, in particular, the preaching. Emerson and Smith found an intriguing fact through their research of television viewing habits of black and white individuals in the mid-1990s. They found that in the mid-1990s the two top-rated television shows for whites were ranked twentieth and eighty-ninth for blacks. The top shows for blacks were one hundred and twenty-second and one hundred and twenty-fourth for whites. They write, "Black and white Americans largely watch and identify with separate stars, shows, humor, drama, and more."[13] This likely extends into every ethnicity in our communities and we would be foolish to somehow think that it does not extend into our churches.

Though these differences will be addressed in later chapters, it is important for the preacher to understand his context and experiences are likely different than those of a different ethnicity or race. Understanding this is the first step in being able to adapt or change our preaching methods so that the gospel is presented unhindered by cultural barriers. This is especially important in a nation that is fractured by violence and racial tension.

There is a shortage of valuable research and literature in this area, especially as it relates to preaching. Books on missions and intercultural communication address many of the barriers in communication (which will be addressed in chapter 3) and many preaching books briefly touch on these

---

12. Emerson and Smith, *Divided By Faith*, 9.
13. Emerson and Smith, *Divided By Faith*, 16.

barriers, so we know they exist. Sermon illustrations, applications, and even how we frame our explanation of the biblical text can hinder someone from grasping the beauty found in the gospel if we do not consider the issues that one may have experienced. Paul understood the importance of knowing his audience in 1 Corinthians 10 when he addressed matters of the conscience in relation to God's glory and the possibility of offending someone. He writes,

> "All things are lawful," but not all things are helpful. "All things are lawful," but not all things build up. Let no one seek his own good, but the good of his neighbor. Eat whatever is sold in the meat market without raising any question on the ground of conscience. For "the earth is the Lord's, and the fullness thereof." If one of the unbelievers invites you to dinner and you are disposed to go, eat whatever is set before you without raising any question on the ground of conscience. But if someone says to you, "This has been offered in sacrifice," then do not eat it, for the sake of the one who informed you, and for the sake of conscience—I do not mean your conscience, but his. For why should my liberty be determined by someone else's conscience? If I partake with thankfulness, why am I denounced because of that for which I give thanks?
>
> So, whether you eat or drink, or whatever you do, do all to the glory of God. Give no offense to Jews or to Greeks or to the church of God, just as I try to please everyone in everything I do, not seeking my own advantage, but that of many, that they may be saved. (1 Corinthians 10:23–33)

That passage is from the man who just two chapters prior spoke of how some weaker brothers may have a problem eating meat that has been offered to idols. Paul, with his vast theological knowledge, could have argued with them, showing them how he was correct, and they were simply being immature. But his focus is not on being right. Instead, he focuses on how he can share the gospel without having anything prevent his audience from hearing it. His response? "If food makes my brother stumble, I will never eat meat, lest I make my brother stumble." (1 Corinthians 8:13)

What does it take to have the mind of Paul in the area of racial and ethnic issues in the local church? I believe that most pastors want to reach as many people as possible and most want to do whatever is necessary to connect with those who do not share their history, ethnicity, and culture. Issues arise, however, because most pastors I have encountered simply do not have the tools necessary to connect well across divides or they just have not been challenged to do so. The purpose of this study is not to be an exhaustive resource, but rather a challenge to pastors to rethink their approach to preaching so that their churches and communities can hear the unchanging gospel in a language they understand.

Why Expository Preaching?

Our preaching can take very different forms, though the best way to faithfully teach God's word in its correct context and framework is through expository preaching. Some take expository preaching to mean pouring over every verse in great detail, missing nothing along the way. This approach might spend weeks covering one verse. Others have taken a broader approach saying that expository preaching is making the main idea of the passage the main idea of the sermon. This approach allows for multiple chapters or even an entire book to be the focus of the sermon.

In his remarkable book *Between Two Worlds*, Anglican John Stott makes the case that all preaching is expository preaching. He argues, "It [expository preaching] refers to the content of the sermon (biblical truth) rather than its style (a running commentary). To expound Scripture is to bring out of the text what is there and expose it to view." He later continued this line of thought by stating, "Whether it [the text] is long or short, our responsibility as expositors is to open it up in such a way that it speaks its message clearly, plainly, accurately, relevantly, without addition, subtraction or falsification." For Stott, the biblical text is "a master which dictates and controls what is said."[14]

One of the criticisms expository preaching faces is that it is merely an academic lecture, going verse by verse to explain the meaning and background of a text. There is a hint of truth in that criticism since there are preachers who are more apt to lecture than preach. The desire to be thorough poses a substantial challenge to those who are convicted to preach expository sermons because the aim is to proclaim truth. Explaining just one verse could take hours and the faithful preacher wants to leave nothing behind.

The pull to pour over every detail in preaching is problematic enough in a homogenous church, where most come from similar backgrounds and education. But what happens when the church is multi-ethnic? How does a preacher faithfully explain the text in a way that everyone will not only

---

14. Stott, *Between Two Worlds*, 125–26.

hear the truth of what the Bible says but also how it points to the gospel in a way they understand?

Even more challenging is the use of application. Some preachers choose to avoid application altogether, saying that explanation is the purpose of preaching and it is the Holy Spirit who applies it to the lives of the listeners.[15] There is a danger in avoiding application because the Bible can easily become academic as the sermon fails to show how the text connects with the lives of the listeners.

If "all Scripture is breathed out by God and profitable for teaching, for reproof, for correction, and for training in righteousness, that the man of God may be complete, equipped for every good work" (2 Tim 3:16–17), then shouldn't we apply it to our lives in order to receive those benefits? How does a two thousand-year-old letter from Paul matter to the people in our churches? This question is what many are asking when they arrive and open up their Bibles. Application should not be the only thing addressed but it must be present in our messages in order to show our listeners that the Bible speaks to them just as much today as it did for the original readers.

Working toward better application in our sermons leads those in a multi-ethnic church setting to ask, "How can we do this?" It is a daunting task, but there are preachers who are doing this well. Most of these preachers will never be known beyond their church and circle of friends, and they are not sacrificing biblical fidelity to reach more people. They are not becoming seeker-driven to ensure that visitors feel welcomed and come back. They are not tickling the ears of those in attendance. These men are faithfully proclaiming the gospel, but they are doing it in such a way that artfully and thoughtfully connects with listeners across ethnic divides. They are "preaching without borders" and we will soon see how they do it and how every preacher can as well.

There are books written covering the difficulties and joys of multi-ethnic preaching, but few give any space to expository preaching. Lutheran researchers James Nieman and Thomas Rogers interviewed pastors from various denominations with all sharing the commonality of preaching to multi-ethnic congregations. Their work noted four speech genres that are effective cross culturally: narrative, images, sayings, and poetic language. Their conclusion was that other styles of preaching may be effective in certain situations but are not used very often. They write, "Most [preachers]

---

15. John MacArthur, "Why Doesn't John MacArthur Add Much Application to His Sermons?"

felt that proposition-driven or definition-laden approaches typical in earlier generations were not useful in multi-ethnic settings. For similar reasons, expository style was only rarely used, although it did have a limited and focused role in certain ethnic communities."[16] Bridging the gap between intercultural communication and expository preaching can be done well, even though previous research has shied away from it.

As we progress, we will seek to answer the questions posed in this chapter. Not all issues can be fully answered in such a short work, but the benefit comes in the preacher working through tough questions about his church and community every week in his study and as he stands in the pulpit. There are no easy solutions but the quest in search of them is what makes all the difference in how our messages are heard and applied in the lives of those for whom we must give an account (Heb 13:17).

How to Read This Study

In chapter 2, I seek to lay out some principles from Scripture for why cross ethnic ministry and preaching are part of God's plan as well as for those who are suffering and hurting due to racism. It is a brief overview, a view from thirty thousand feet, but it does serve as a launching pad for other biblical studies that deal with race and ethnicity.

Chapter 3 covers intercultural communication, which is encouraged in evangelism and missions, but, in my experience, is often overlooked in the field of preaching. My hope is this chapter, and the ones following, will show how preachers *must* not only understand their audience, but also be willing to make difficult changes in sermon preparation and delivery. Also discussed are some examples of how intercultural communication is difficult, but how it becomes even more difficult in the life of the local church.

Chapter 4 is really the heart of this study. In this chapter, I will explain what the gospel is and how understanding it will change everything that we say from the pulpit. In this chapter I will address issues that seem to divide Christians: racism and social justice. To be clear, this study is not a work about those topics, but they are topics pastors of multi-ethnic churches find themselves discussing often. In other words, they cannot be ignored. The primary purpose of this chapter is to show how the gospel touches on the issues about which Christians can never seem to agree.

---

16. Nieman and Rogers, *Preaching to Every Pew*, 47.

Preaching without Borders

In chapter 5, we will see how expository preaching fits into a church with a multi-ethnic congregation. The concept of, and the commitment to, expository preaching will be examined. Examples of expository preaching will be presented, comparing how expositors in different parts of the country, with different congregations, handle certain texts of Scripture. The most important aspect of this chapter is a discussion of how the gospel applies to the problems that come from being a part of a multi-ethnic church. Chapter 6 adds onto the framework built in chapter 5 by addressing the possibilities of expository preaching in a multiethnic church. In other words, how do we take a passage written two thousand years ago to a certain group of people and proclaim it today to listeners who come from different backgrounds, nations, and experiences?

To use an aeronautical term, chapter 7 begins our "descent" by asking the question, "What happens if we don't adapt?" This chapter addresses the consequences of both failing to acknowledge our shortcomings and neglecting to act, both in the present and in the years to come. If chapter 7 begins the "descent," chapter 8 is the landing. Throughout the study, I have attempted to show the biblical basis for expository preaching and for building a ministry that welcomes and celebrates people from every ethnicity and background. In chapter 8, I wrap everything up with a challenge to improve as expositors of both the Scripture and of our church and community.

I am the first to admit I do not have all the answers. As you continue to read this study, you will quickly see that I am not an expert, but I have found the lessons learned through careful study of the Bible, the church, and the community have had a glorious effect on the quality of my preaching. I am much more equipped to preach God's word to people who are different from me and, because of that, I am a better pastor.

My hope is to challenge pastors to consider the hard task of preaching outside of their comfort zone. I will be honest: I'm not very good at this. I want an easy road, a path void of thorns and thistles. I do not want to face criticism or conflict. I want an easy life and an easy ministry but, in all my study of the Bible, I have yet to find a place where we are told that our lives will be easy. This study gives no easy answers, but it is my prayer that the reader will be challenged to think more deeply about how to present the truth of God's word.

2

Building a Cross-Ethnic Ministerial Philosophy

Perhaps the reason we do not hear much about multi-ethnic preaching is because it is not directly addressed in the Bible, though we certainly see examples of preaching and sharing the gospel cross-ethnically. There are a number of passages which give us examples of preaching, though compared to other theological doctrines, the total number is relatively small. However, we can quickly build a theological framework to assist us in our task of preaching Christ and him crucified.

Every Person Has Worth

The truth of a person having worth often gets confused with someone having self-esteem. Self-esteem comes when a girl believes she is pretty because of what those around her tell her. But this will fade as she ages with the wrinkles and grey hair that are part of the maturation process. Nowhere in Scripture are we instructed to view ourselves highly but we do see a theme running through the Bible that we have worth because God says we do, and because we are created with special attributes that God only gave to human beings. Those two facts alone should be more than enough to convince even the most skeptical that every human being has innate worth.

Preaching without Borders

The Bible absolutely affirms the worth of human beings. In the first chapter of Genesis we see God stating our worth: "Then God said, 'Let us make man in our image, after our likeness . . . So God created man in his own image, in the image of God he created him; male and female he created them" (Gen 1:26–27). Our worth is not from anything we have done or can do, but solely on what God has already done for us.

We see in Psalm 139 that God formed our inward parts and he knit us together in our mother's womb. There is no racial or ethnic qualification for this. There is no divide between histories or backgrounds. We are all created in the image of God, but that is not where we should stop in our understanding of our worth. For the Christian, not only have we been created in the image of God, but we have also been born again in the likeness of Christ. If we cannot see the worth in every human being simply based on their humanity, we must see value in our own brothers and sisters!

In response to a lawyer asking how he can inherit eternal life, found in Luke 10:25–37, Jesus says, "You shall love the Lord your God will all your heart and with all your soul and with all your strength and with all your mind, and your neighbor as yourself." The lawyer certainly understood the first part as he was familiar with the *shema* found in Deuteronomy 6, but he found it difficult to define who exactly was his neighbor. Then Jesus proceeds to give him the parable:

> A man was going down from Jerusalem to Jericho, and he fell among robbers, who stripped him and beat him and departed, leaving him half dead. Now by chance a priest was going down that road, and when he saw him he passed by on the other side. So likewise a Levite, when he came to the place and saw him, passed by on the other side. But a Samaritan, as he journeyed, came to where he was, and when he saw him, he had compassion. He went to him and bound up his wounds, pouring on oil and wine. Then he set him on his own animal and brought him to an inn and took care of him. And the next day he took out two denarii and gave them to the innkeeper, saying, 'Take care of him, and whatever more you spend, I will repay you when I come back.' Which of these three, do you think, proved to be a neighbor to the man who fell among the robbers? He said, 'The one who showed him mercy.' And Jesus said to him, 'You go, and do likewise.' (Luke 10:30–37)

The first person who walked by the injured man was a priest who walked across the road to avoid the man who desperately needed help. There is no reason given but it is clear that someone well-versed in Old

Testament Scripture would have remembered passages that command Jews to help those in need. Regardless, the priest refused to help. The next person passing by was a Levite, an assistant to the priest in the temple. Like the priest before him, the Levite moved to the opposite side of the road and offered no help.

Then a Samaritan comes to the scene. Bock notes, "For a Jew, a Samaritan was among the least respected of people. Eating with Samaritans was equated with eating pork. Such people were unclean and to be avoided. The Samaritan would be the last type of person the lawyer would expect to be the climactic figure who resolves the story."[1] The Samaritan did not call for help. Instead, he bound up his wounds, poured oil and wine over the cuts, brought the man to the inn, and took care of him. The next day he promised to pay any bills the man would incur.

In this parable one would expect a Jew to be the hero, but Jesus makes the Samaritan, not the Jew, the hero. Samaritans were hated by Jews, and Jesus deliberately chose one, an outsider, to be the hero of his parable to show that being a good neighbor is not a matter of nationality or race.[2] What a person is does not matter because every person was created in the image of God and thus has worth to both God and to the children of God.

God So Loved the World

The re-creation and adoption of the elect into the family of God was not reserved only for the Jews or any other group alone. The most famous verse of the Bible, John 3:16, not only speaks about what God has done but it also speaks to whom God gives eternal life. We can quickly reject the notion that this verse supports universalism, that all will one day be saved, due to the overwhelming evidence in the rest of Scripture that denies universal salvation. But we cannot overlook the use of the word *kosmos*, especially in our study of multi-ethnic preaching.

For Jews who were familiar with the Old Testament prophecies, it was well understood that salvation would come from their family tree. The Messiah would one day come and rescue his people from their bondage. But according to John 3:16 (and 1 John 2:2, among others), salvation did not belong to the Jews alone. It now belonged to the world, including those outside of Judaism. Carson concludes, "It is clear that it is atypical for John

1. Bock, *Luke*, 1031.
2. Stein, *Luke*, 317–18.

to speak of God's love for *the world*, but this truth is therefore made to stand out as all the more wonderful. Jews were familiar with the truth that God loved the children of Israel; here God's love is not restricted by race."[3] Köstenberger echoes Carson: "Significantly, God's love extends not merely to Israel, but to 'the world,' that is, sinful humanity. Just as God's love encompasses the entire world, so Jesus made atonement for the sins of the whole world."[4]

The idea that God loves those outside of Judaism is not only found in John's writing but also in Paul's. In Rom 15:8–12, we read:

> For I tell you that Christ became a servant to the circumcised to show God's truthfulness, in order to confirm the promises given to the patriarchs, and in order that the Gentiles might glorify God for his mercy. As it is written,
>
> 'Therefore I will praise you among the Gentiles, and sing to your name.'
>
> And again it is said,
> 'Rejoice, O Gentiles, with his people.'
>
> And again,
> 'Praise the Lord, all you Gentiles,
>   and let all the peoples extol him.'
>
> And again Isaiah says,
> 'The root of Jesse will come,
>   even he who arises to rule the Gentiles;
> in him will the Gentiles hope.'

Though this passage has references that some may not quickly grasp, Paul's point is that Jesus came for both Jews and Gentiles. The first Christians were Jews, as was Jesus, but it was never God's plan for salvation to belong only to the Jews. Schreiner observes,

> The fulfillment of the promises to the fathers does not exclude the Gentiles but includes them, for the covenant with the fathers from its inception pledged that 'all nations' would receive God's blessing (Gen 12:3; 18:18; 22:18; 26:4). By definition, then, the fulfillment of the promise to the fathers widens the circle for the whole world. This is certainly Paul's understanding of the promise;

---

3. Carson, *Gospel According to John*, 205.
4. Köstenberger, *John*, 129.

Abraham is 'heir of the world' (Rom. 4:13), and thus the father of Jews and Gentiles (4:9–17). Christ's purpose in coming, then, was not only to certify the promises to the Jews, but also to include the Gentiles in the circle of his mercy. The word "mercy" (ἐλέους, *eleous*) resounds with covenantal overtones, harking back to God's חֶסֶד (*hesed*, loyal love), which, though not identical with God's covenant, is closely tied to it in the OT. The Gentiles glorify God for his covenantal mercy. That is, they praise God because they were the undeserved recipients of his saving kindness. Since both Jews and Gentiles have been blessed in such a singular way, they should extend acceptance to those in the community who differ from themselves.[5]

As previously stated, race and ethnicity have no bearing on one's worth. Jesus came to live and die for people of every race, ethnicity, gender, background, disability, preference, socio-economic status, age, or anything else that we use to classify and divide ourselves. This is echoed in John's vision in Revelation:

> "Worthy are you to take the scroll
>   and to open its seals,
> for you were slain, and by your blood you ransomed people for God
>   from every tribe and language and people and nation,
> and you have made them a kingdom and priests to our God,
>   and they shall reign on the earth."

The gospel reaches across tribes, languages, and nations to unite the elect of God into a kingdom of priests.

No Divisions

In a text that most Christians quickly recognize, the Apostle Paul writes in 1 Corinthians 1:10–13,

> I appeal to you, brothers, by the name of our Lord Jesus Christ, that all of you agree, and that there be no divisions among you, but that you be united in the same mind and the same judgment. For it has been reported to me by Chloe's people that there is quarreling among you, my brothers. What I mean is that each one of you says, "I follow Paul," or "I follow Apollos," or "I follow Cephas," or

---

5. Schreiner, *Romans*, 756.

"I follow Christ." Is Christ divided? Was Paul crucified for you? Or were you baptized in the name of Paul?

According to Richards and O'Brien, what westerners often think when they read this passage is that there were issues regarding theology or devotion to different personalities. Richards and O'Brien believe that there is something else happening in the church in Corinth. They write,

> We may be failing to note ethnic markers that Paul sprinkled all over the text. Apollos was noted as an Alexandrian (Egyptian) Jew (Acts 18:24). They had their own reputation. Paul notes that Peter is called by his Aramaic name, Cephas, suggesting the group that followed him spoke Aramaic and were thus Palestinian Jews. Paul's church had Diaspora Jews but also many ethnic Corinthians, who were quite proud of their status as residents of a Roman colony and who enjoyed using Latin. This may explain why Paul doesn't address any theological differences. There weren't any. The problem was ethnic division: Aramaic-speaking Jews, Greek-speaking Jews, Romans and Alexandrians.[6]

Though Paul does not mention the reason behind the disputes in the church, Richards and O'Brien believe that ethnicity may very well have been the reason behind the factions. Garland notes that the differences in the church cannot be attributed to theological differences because Paul himself encourages division when something contradicted the gospel. According to Garland, what bothered Paul the most was how brothers and sisters were alienating themselves from one another. He notes, "This conclusion does not mean that their theology is not distorted. As Paul evaluates the situation, they have exchanged the wisdom of the cross for delusive, worldly wisdom."[7] It was likely not an issue over essential theological issues, but rather something else.

If Richards and O'Brien are correct, we must, as westerners, begin asking ourselves how much of our interpretations are built on western thought rather than how the original readers would have interpreted the text. This issue of culture affecting interpretation will be addressed much more as we progress.

---

6. Richards and O'Brien, *Misreading Scripture with Western Eyes*, 66.
7. Garland, *1 Corinthians*, 50.

Building a Cross-Ethnic Ministerial Philosophy

Hope for Those Suffering Injustice and Racism

As we will discuss throughout this book and particularly in chapter four, the Bible contains many examples that non-white preachers have used as a way to encourage their people and to give them hope in times of suffering and injustice. The Gospel of Matthew records the events of the Magi travelling from Asia to Bethlehem to bring gifts to Jesus. DeYoung, et al., note that this story was an "allusion to the Gentile inclusion in God's salvation story." They then discuss the events leading to Mary, Joseph, and Jesus being forced to flee to Egypt for a few years. In their study of black preachers and their own anecdotal accounts, they have found, "Many African American preachers and others have used this passage to annul the message of white racists—'Out of Africa I have called my son.'"[8] As a white preacher who grew up in white churches, I have missed how this application can help our black brothers and sisters see the connection that they have with the person of Christ.

What I have seen in my own church life, books that I have read, and pastors that I have had fellowship with, is a blindness to the viewpoints and perspectives of others. To be fair, everyone at times can be blinded by their own experiences and upbringing to the point where they fail to question how someone else may interpret, view, apply, or feel about a particular issue. It has been my experience that what is true for me is likely true for most white Christians and pastors in the United States. I vividly recall how many of my white friends complained about Black History Month or anything that they viewed as racially divisive. To them, speaking about race only caused harm to society. To them, it was something we've "moved past," not something that needed to be addressed in our "advanced" culture.

This will be addressed in nearly every following chapter, but it fits well into this discussion about how the Bible addresses race, ethnicity, and hope because it is something to which most white Christians have never been exposed. Carl Ellis summarizes how poorly the history of Africans in the church has been communicated. He attests,

> As Jesus was carrying his cross through the streets of Jerusalem, he stumbled under its weight. Simon, a black man from Cyrene, Africa, was enlisted to carry the cross the rest of the way (Luke 23:36). On the day of Pentecost, people from every nation (including African nations) heard the gospel and were converted (Acts 2:5–12).

---

8. DeYoung, et al., *United By Faith*, 14.

> An Ethiopian government official was converted on his way home (Acts 8:26–39). The church at Antioch had several African members, among them two prophets or teachers: Simeon, called the black man, and Lucius the Cyrenian (Acts 13:1). What were those two Africans doing in Antioch? We find in Acts 11:19–21 that they had gone there when they learned that non-Jews were not hearing the good news from the Jewish missionaries; the young African church may have been sending missionaries like Simeon and Lucius to plant churches. It was out of that Antioch church that Paul and Barnabas were sent to evangelize Turkey, Greece, and Italy. So the European church partly has the African church to thank for its missionary faithfulness.[9]

How many white preachers have considered the impact that Africa has had in Christian history? How many, outside of a church history class, recognize that Athanasius (Egypt) and Augustine (present-day Algeria) were both African? And how many black brothers and sisters have heard the hope that comes from Christ who himself has a history on the continent?

The same could be said about every culture and background. Many in our churches find no real, tangible connection with the people in Scripture and this is a problem that is rarely addressed. By knowing the Bible and the movement of God throughout history, coupled with a knowledge of world history, preachers will be able to show their people that those who look like them have had an impact on the spread of the gospel.

Ethnic Diversity in Preaching

Ethnic diversity in the church is neither a fad nor is it something pastors and theologians have concocted on their own. Support for this is taken directly from Scripture. If all humans have worth because we were created in the image of God and Jesus died for both Jew and Gentile, how can we come to any other conclusion than God desires churches to be multi-ethnic, reflecting the communities in which they are located?

A look at the New Testament shows examples of ethnic diversity in the delivery of the gospel. In Acts 10, we see how the early church shared the gospel with those outside of the Jewish family:

> So Peter opened his mouth and said: "Truly I understand that God shows no partiality, but in every nation anyone who fears him and

---

9. Ellis, Jr., *Free at Last?*, 39.

does what is right is acceptable to him. As for the word that he sent to Israel, preaching good news of peace through Jesus Christ (he is Lord of all), you yourselves know what happened throughout all Judea, beginning from Galilee after the baptism that John proclaimed: how God anointed Jesus of Nazareth with the Holy Spirit and with power. He went about doing good and healing all who were oppressed by the devil, for God was with him. And we are witnesses of all that he did both in the country of the Jews and in Jerusalem. They put him to death by hanging him on a tree, but God raised him on the third day and made him to appear, not to all the people but to us who had been chosen by God as witnesses, who ate and drank with him after he rose from the dead. And he commanded us to preach to the people and to testify that he is the one appointed by God to be judge of the living and the dead. To him all the prophets bear witness that everyone who believes in him receives forgiveness of sins through his name." (Acts 10:34–43)

Peter's gospel presentation is an example that God does not show partiality regarding whom he chooses. One's nationality, ethnicity, or race has no bearing on God's sovereign election. He chooses from every tribe, nation, and tongue so naturally our churches should serve as examples of this borderless faith. The barrier has been removed between the nation of Israel and the Gentiles.[10] Polhill notes that this sermon from Peter follows the pattern of his earlier sermons to the Jews but with some differences. He explains, "One is found at the very outset, where he stressed that God shows no favoritism, accepts people from every nation, and that Jesus is 'Lord of all.' This emphasis on the universal gospel is particularly suited to a message to Gentiles." There are now no divisions between clean and unclean people from God's perspective.[11]

Peter's example is one for those who preach to multi-ethnic audiences. Rather than addressing the Jewish belief system as the foundation for Christianity, he instead focuses on the fact that God shows no favoritism. His listeners may have understood how God chose Israel to be his people in the Old Testament, but they needed to hear how Israel is really found in Jesus and all people can come to him for salvation through faith. He did not change the gospel; instead, he contextualized it, sharing the message in a way which helped the listeners connect the story to their own lives and ethnic history.

10. Kistemaker and Hendriksen, *Exposition of the Acts of the Apostles*, 392.
11. Polhill, *Acts*, 260.

Preaching without Borders

In chapter 13 of Acts, we find Paul giving an example of apologetic preaching, though the method is quite different from Peter just a few chapters prior. Paul's audience was mixed, and the Gentiles were so moved by Paul's message that they became Christians. As one commentator noted, "These people realized that the Christian faith was based on the Old Testament Scriptures but was free from the demands placed on them by the Jews."[12] Though Paul was preaching the same gospel as Peter, it is clear that their messages fit their context. Paul was addressing Jews as well as men "who fear God." He was speaking to both Jew and Gentile, yet his message was clear to both. He did not have to water down the gospel, nor did he feel the need to leave out essential truths in order to convince those unfamiliar with Jewish Scripture.

In Acts 14 and 17, Paul is preaching to a Gentile audience. In chapter 14 Paul and Barnabas are in Lystra, where they heal a crippled man, and after this, the crowds said (in their own language), "The gods have come down to us in the likeness of men!" When Paul and Barnabas heard that they were being viewed as Hermes and Zeus, respectively, they rushed to the crowd and began preaching. Paul did not appeal to their understanding of Jewish Scripture because they likely had none. Instead, he appealed to them by speaking of how God created things. He said, "In past generations he allowed all the nations to walk in their own ways. Yet he did not leave himself without witness, for he did good by giving you rains from heaven and fruitful seasons, satisfying your hearts with food and gladness." (Acts 14:16–17) Paul and Barnabas were obviously not able to give a full gospel presentation, only referencing the basic understanding that there is only one God. However, Paul's message to the people serves us today as an example to follow; he knew that the people needed the basics before anything else. Based on Paul's other messages, it is likely that, given the time, Paul would have presented the full gospel to those in Lystra.

In Paul's letter to the Church in Galatia, he writes, "For as many of you as were baptized into Christ have put on Christ. There is neither Jew nor Greek, there is neither slave nor free, there is no male and female, for you are all one in Christ Jesus." (Gal 3:27–28) The ethnic tension in the church was clear to Paul as he wrote this letter to convince the church to love and honor one another as brothers and sisters. Their identity in Christ superseded every previous identity they may have held. Kistemaker and Hendriksen note this tension: "It seems that the Judaizers of Paul's day had

---

12. Kistemaker and Hendriksen, *Exposition of the Acts of the Apostles*, 468.

not broken away from this feeling of disdain for non-Jews. Gentiles, too, were often guilty of similar snobbery. They looked down upon the Jews as much as the latter looked down upon them."[13]

Conclusion

All of this has tremendous implications for us in our preaching. First, we must recognize that every person listening to us preach has value and is made in God's image. Second, those who hear us and are Christians are our brothers and sisters. They are more than a warm body, a giver, or a volunteer. They are our kin and just as we would do anything for our blood family, we must be willing to do anything for our spiritual family. I once heard a pastor say that we have more in common with our Christian brethren thousands of miles away than we do with our blood relatives who do not know Christ. That is all the more powerful when considered within the local church family. Third, if the first two implications are true, then every preacher *must* preach in such a way that respects his listeners. The difficulty comes when a preacher comprehends what he should do but does not have the tools, resources, or experiences to allow him to do so. Continue reading and you will find hope that every gospel-centered preacher is able to accomplish this challenging task!

---

13. Hendriksen and Kistemaker, *Exposition of Galatians*, 150.

3

Intercultural Communication at Work

I AM GUILTY OF expecting everyone to be like me. Many of us are that way too. We set the standard in our minds of what is right, wrong, or neutral, and we expect others to live and believe within the ethical and moral framework that we've created. Most of my pastor friends would, at least at first, recoil at a statement like that but I think they would agree after some thought. Why? Because I like it when my leadership and preaching come easy. It's nice to study a text all week with minimal study of my congregation and my community.

In the first two chapters, we've seen how there is a need for preachers to be aware of their congregation—both what it currently looks like as well as what we hope it looks like in the future, based on the demographics of the community. We saw how cities are changing and becoming more diverse and why it is important for preachers to pay attention to these trends. We also covered some key biblical texts that show that ethnic and cultural diversity is a positive thing. In this chapter, I will show how intercultural communication is not something best left to a college classroom. It is practical for the preacher because a preacher needs to speak the language—tone, rhythm, cadence, and hidden meanings—of his listeners.

Intercultural Communication at Work

This Is Hard Work

Here is what I've found to be true in my ministry: it is much easier to preach to people who are just like me. If everyone in my congregation looked the same, came from the same socio-economic situation, voted the same way, and had the same convictions about what Scripture says and how to apply it, my job as a pastor and teacher would be much easier. I wouldn't have to carefully and prayerfully craft my words because there would be no controversy no matter what I said.

But there are always differences in the church. A church that is 100 percent Anglo, Republican, and middle class will still have differences in theology, how to raise children, and what kind of music is best for corporate worship. But those are often front and center, and a pastor who pays attention will be able to navigate through those difficult subjects. It is more difficult to discern how someone's ancestry affects how they view the world or how being raised in a certain part of the world gives a person a very different outlook on religion, family, and nearly everything else.

A preacher needs to have multiple tools in his toolbox if he is to successfully communicate the unchanging gospel to a rapidly changing world. In addition to knowing Scripture, the preacher must be able to know his community—where they come from, what makes them tick, and what their traditions represent.

Why Cultural Intelligence Is Necessary

I had never heard of the term *cultural intelligence* until recently, but it's a concept that has become indispensable in my sermon preparation and delivery. So, what does *cultural intelligence* mean? First, it's important to understand what culture is. Matthew Kim defines culture this way: "Culture is a group's way of living, way of thinking, and way of behaving in the world, for which we need understanding and empathy to guide listeners toward Christian maturity."[1] That said, cultural intelligence is knowing the history and experiences of a community, both inside and out of the church. The challenge before every preacher is, to use the words of John Stott, to preach between two worlds, only in the case of a multi-ethnic congregation, the preacher may find himself between dozens of different worlds.

---

1. Kim, *Preaching with Cultural Intelligence*, 5.

Preaching without Borders

What happens to a church when the ethnic demographic of the neighborhood changes? Some may say that preaching the Word is enough and I would agree that we are to preach the Word in season and out of season. But shouldn't every pastor know his audience in addition to knowing and preaching the Word? Duane Elmer says that being able to communicate across cultures is a survival skill. He argues, "If I am willing to pay the price to learn another's cultural frame of reference, I can avoid many conflicts—and in the end, I will find myself the richer for it. In fact, we all need to gain understanding of other cultures, even if we never plan to leave the country we were born in."[2]

Conflict will come when cultures intersect, but it isn't just conflict that we're trying to avoid. Our entire purpose is to make disciples so we should seek to remove impediments to being obedient to the Great Commission. Ridding our preaching of unnecessary barriers to someone hearing and applying the gospel should be our aim, but that requires effort.

Kim, whose book is aptly titled *Preaching with Cultural Intelligence*, discusses key differences between western and Asian preaching. He states that few attempts have been made to erase borders in our preaching.

> Yet it is in the purview of every culturally intelligent preacher to unmask and sympathize with our listeners who have experienced deep-seated wounds as minority group members and to provide avenues for authentic healing and reconciliation, especially with injuries from the dominant culture. While I acknowledge that real theological differences exist and elements of non-Western theologies are biblically misaligned, our cultural intelligence engages in active listening to place ourselves in the shoes of those who have encountered discrimination and affliction on account of their race and ethnicity and to identify with their pain.[3]

What does an Anglo preacher do when the area around his church changes? How can he effectively preach the word through exegesis and application if he does not have a grasp on not only the needs of his community but also its history?

Pastors who don't care about the experiences and histories of those unlike them exist, though their scope of influence is limited to a small corner of the internet. Those I encounter are very interested in connecting with the community in their preaching, but we are most comfortable with those like

---

2. Elmer, *Cross-Cultural Conflict*, 13.
3. Kim, *Preaching with Cultural Intelligence*, 106.

us. That may not matter as much in a rural community in Nebraska, but the demographics in many places are changing. David Helm, who pastors in one of the most racially diverse neighborhoods in Chicago, maintains:

> The congregations to which many of us are preaching will be, by nature, more diverse in background and replete with competing worldviews that—if we are not careful with our words—could be an unnecessary cause of combustion. Our preaching should have a more diverse audience in mind, which means we should be willing to trade in the colloquialisms and inside jokes of our own little subcultures. You wouldn't address the city council with the same stories you would tell a close friend over lunch. It's a matter of re-orienting our scope. We should preach as though we intend to be understood by people from the four corners of the earth precisely because, in many cases, those will be the people within the sound of our voice.[4]

Cultural intelligence gives the preacher the ability to reach more people with the gospel. We not only need to exegete Scripture, we need to exegete our audience.

More Than Words

I started at a new school in my junior year of high school. During my first visit to the school, I spent some time with the guidance counselor who helped me pick out my elective classes. There was art and music and a few others, but she immediately said how much I would like a class called Visual Language. I've blocked out most of my memories from that time, but I fondly remember that class. Mr. V. was the teacher and he made class seem less like school and more like a visit to your favorite museum. Above all the fun projects we were able to do (making movie trailers and stop-motion animations), Mr. V. taught me that communication is more than just words on a piece of paper or a sermon out of the mouth of the pastor. Yes, words have meaning. That's the easiest thing about communication. But what about the words *behind* the words? In *Folly, Grace, and Power: The Mysterious Act of Preaching*, John Koessler adds, "Language is a basic component of human culture. The peculiar accent of one's native tongue is more than a

---

4. Helm, *Expositional Preaching*, 92.

collection of sounds arranged in distinct patterns; it is also a way of looking at the world and organizing ideas."[5]

Words have meaning, but meaning comes from what the listener thinks the word means. An example of this happened in my childhood where the word *bad* mostly meant something undesirable, but *bad* also meant *good*, as in something cool. An older woman might call a disruptive, disobedient child *bad*, which would fit in the normal use of the word, but a group of kids might use the same word for a kid wearing a new pair of basketball shoes. The words they use require knowledge of their culture. I have had to pay close attention to my use of words in my context because I have newborns and folks in their nineties in our church. Saying that something is *bad* in a certain way would certainly elicit stares from nearly everyone but children of the eighties.

What I mean by all this is that ideas come from our cultural experiences. Shuang, Volcic, and Gallois give an example of this. They discuss how different indirect and direct communications styles are. Westerners typically prefer direct communication, where "the speaker's needs, wants, desires, and intentions are explicitly communicated." Indirect communication, favored by collectivist cultures and most Asian cultures, is a style where "the speaker's true intentions or needs are only implied or hinted at during conversation." The authors give an example using an American and a Nigerian:

> An American student asked his Nigerian friend to give him a lift on an evening when the Nigerian had made a commitment to babysit his niece so that his sister could go to work. However, instead of saying, 'Sorry I cannot do it,' he replied by talking about how his sister perhaps could make alternative arrangements or stay home instead of working that night. The American student felt confused as to what his Nigerian friend was trying to say. In American culture, if such a request for a lift is inconvenient, one would simply respond by saying, 'Sorry, I cannot do it.' However, in collectivistic cultures like Nigeria, it is not considered polite to say 'no' to a friend—but it is the responsibility of the person who made the request to figure out it is not appropriate to ask for the favour. Therefore differences in expectations for appropriate communication styles can lead to misunderstandings between speakers.[6]

---

5. Koessler, *Folly, Grace, and Power*, 86.
6. Liu, Volcic, and Gallois, *Introducing Intercultural Communication*, 128–29.

Richards and O'Brien discuss something similar to the above example. They cite a study where the researcher had twelve American seminary students read the Parable of the Prodigal Son in Luke 15 and then retell it as well as they could. None of the twelve students mentioned the famine in Luke 15:14. The researcher wanted a larger sample size, so he chose one hundred people to read the passage and retell the story as accurately as possible. Only six of the participants mentioned the famine. It is important to note that the hundred participants were very diverse, but they were all Americans. The researcher then tried the experiment again, only this time there were fifty participants and they all lived in St. Petersburg, Russia. Forty-two of the fifty participants mentioned the famine. Richards and O'Brien write,

> Why? Just seventy years before, 670,000 people had died of starvation after a Nazi German siege of the capital city began a three-year famine. Famine was very much a part of the history and imagination of the Russian participants in [the] exercise. Based solely on cultural location, people from America and Russia disagreed about what they considered the crucial details of the story.[7]

Seven decades passed and the people participating in the study still remembered their shared history. Both the American and the Russian participants read the same passage and were asked the same questions, but the answers they gave were very different.

Cultural Differences

When I began my preaching ministry, I assumed that as long as I knew the gospel and preached it, my preaching would see spiritual growth and my ministry would flourish. I quickly learned that I could preach *at* people very easily but preaching *to* them was an altogether different story. I fell flat because I was paying no attention to the people who were in my congregation. I didn't know enough about the people God had entrusted to me and it showed in my preaching.

Each culture has things that make it unique. Some things are easy to discern: food, weather, or skin color. But the more important things go much deeper. Things like shame culture, shared experiences, or achievement culture all require tools for navigating through. Tim Keller pastored

---

7. Richards and O'Brien, *Misreading Scripture with Western Eyes*, 14.

Redeemer Presbyterian Church in New York City for nearly three decades. In his book *Preaching*, he gives an example of a situation he faced:

> Here's an example from my own ministry. Many Christians in my congregation are Asian and feel quite pressured by parental expectations to achieve and succeed. They often feel they are failing their parents. However, many young Anglo professionals in our church have grown up in a much more individualistic culture and in many ways struggle with anger and bitterness toward parents they feel have let them down and failed them.[8]

That echoes my own experience. So, what is a preacher to do? We can continue to preach from our own perspective but that doesn't satisfy because we've made it difficult for a large and growing portion of the population to connect with our preaching. Keller rhetorically asks the question and then answers it himself:

> How might I address this range of motivations in a single sermon? By reminding them that the only parental love you can't lose, and the only parental love you must have, is found in the ultimate, heavenly Father, who secured us through the saving work of Jesus Christ. Even though he was God's Son, he was cast out and lost, so that you could be brought in to the family of God. When you realize that he did that for you, the love of the Father becomes the most precious and real thing to you. When that happens, if you are bitter because you didn't get your parents' love, you can afford to forgive them, because they haven't impoverished you; you are rich in parental love. And those of you feeling like failures before your parents' expectations can relax, because you have the approval of the only Father whose opinion counts.[9]

If we didn't know about shame culture that is part of many Asian communities or how many Asian-Americans are raised with heavy pressure from their family to succeed, we would miss out on an opportunity to apply the gospel directly to their own experience.

Everyone has opinions and it's only natural to become irritated or frustrated when what we think is right clashes with what another person believes is right. This is true for political discussions at Thanksgiving as well as how the church should be run or what style of preaching the pastor should adopt. No matter the situation we find ourselves in, our past and

---

8. Keller, *Preaching*, 119.
9. Keller, *Preaching*, 119–20.

our own biases will take control over what we say if we aren't careful. Lingenfelter and Mayers write that knowing our own cultural bias is essential for effective ministry. They write, "Once we have understood the power of our cultural habits over us, we are more ready to call on the spiritual power and freedom we enjoy in Christ to break the habits of our culture, to let go of them, and to enter into another culture to help those people encounter Christ."[10] Tom Nichols, an expert in international relations, asserts that we have "an inherent and natural tendency to search for evidence that already meshes with our beliefs. Our brains are actually wired this way, which is why we argue even when we shouldn't. And if we feel socially or personally threatened, we will argue until we're blue in the face."[11] Nichols is not a professed evangelical but he understands how difficult it is to communicate well across cultures.

Richards and O'Brien give an example in their work about how the individualistic culture of the United States struggles to understand other cultures who think differently. They write:

> The person's identity comes by distinguishing herself from the people around her. She is encouraged to avoid peer pressure and be an independent thinker. She will make her decisions regardless of what others think; she may defy her parents with her choice of a college major or career or spouse. The highest goal and virtue in this sort of culture is being true to oneself. The supreme value is the sovereignty of the individual.[12]

That describes an aspect of what most Americans love about their country: rugged, resilient, and defiant individualism. *No one can tell me what to do. I will do what is right for me.* Parents, siblings, extended family, friends, co-workers, neighbors, and fellow church members certainly factor into our decisions, but they will never be more important than what we think is best for us. But the dominance of Anglo-American culture is declining with the growth of immigration and the rising birth rate of those who are currently minorities.

The growing diversity we see in the United States means that different cultures will have to live together or there will be conflict. Embracing the differences as gifts from God goes a long way in our individual stories and in our preaching; embracing different cultural experiences helps us

---

10. Lingenfelter and Mayers, *Ministering Cross-Culturally*, 12.
11. Nichols, *Death of Expertise*, 41.
12. Richards and O'Brien, *Misreading Scripture with Western Eyes*, 96.

to present the gospel in a language the different listeners can understand. Richards and O'Brien use their own experiences on the mission field in a culture that valued the collective over the individual. They write:

> Collectivist cultures are very different indeed. In a collectivist culture, the most important entity is the community—the family, the tribe or the county—and *not* the individual. Preserving the harmony of the community is everyone's primary goal, and is perceived as much more important than the self-expression or self-fulfillment of the individual. A person's identity comes not from distinguishing himself from the community, but in knowing and faithfully fulfilling his place. One's goal is not to get ahead or move beyond one's community; after all, "the tallest blade of grass is cut first." Rather, members of collectivist cultures make decisions based on the counsel of elders—parents, aunts or uncles. The highest goal and virtue in this sort of culture is supporting the community.[13]

Along the same lines as the previous quote about collectivist cultures, Richards and O'Brien discuss how shame cultures dictate how people make decisions. They write that in these cultures people are pressured to obey because if they don't, they will face the shame of their community. Those who were raised in the West and who have family histories deeply rooted in western thinking will not naturally think community first. In their study of Hispanic preaching, Justo González and Pablo Jiménez write about how the family is central to their churches and to their preaching. They write that in Anglo culture, the family is closed and distinguished from all other groups. The immediate family comes first. Hispanic families, however, are different. They write:

> The family is an extensive reality, fluid, with imprecise limits, which includes relatives and connections in all sorts of degrees of consanguinity. It is even possible and almost inevitable to belong to more than one family. Therefore, when in the dominant culture one speaks of the relationship between family and church, the church is seen as an aggregate of families, just as society is an aggregate of individuals. In contrast, in Hispanic culture the church is a family. This is reinforced by the fact that many among our people, used as they are to extended families of their countries of origin, feel a deep need for the sort and quality of relationships that such a

---

13. Richards and O'Brien, *Misreading Scripture with Western Eyes*, 97.

family offers. Perhaps it is our task to rediscover and redefine the meaning of the affirmation that the church is the family of God.[14]

What happens when the individualistic culture of white western families collide with our Hispanic brothers and sisters who view family as a much larger entity? When the priorities and allegiances are defined differently, it is inevitable that some conflict will arise. As the primary leader of the church from the pulpit, the preacher must craft his words so that the church is shown how the gospel doesn't eliminate our uniqueness, but that it does tear down walls that we have built up. The only way for anyone to know how to clear those walls is through studying the various cultures in our church families and in the surrounding community.

Having cultural intelligence—knowing those hearing our sermon—means that we aren't putting up unnecessary roadblocks which prevent people from hearing the gospel above all else. Now take that pressure of high expectations and combine it with the individualism of Anglo America, the strong emphasis on family from many Central and South American cultures, the collectivist culture of Africa, and the shame-dominated cultures found in Asia, and you have a powder keg of United Nations proportions! What the preacher must do is know the various cultures, consider the cultures, and communicate to the cultures.

Honoring One Another

Embracing our differences in the church and celebrating the beautiful tapestry that God has created is important for our Christian witness and for our growth in holiness. But we cannot embrace our differences if we do not honor one another. I was born during the early days of the Reagan Administration, so I don't have first-hand knowledge of what the political world looked like. But much of my time in college was spent studying political science with an emphasis on political history in the United States. I should not have been surprised to learn that political campaigns have always contained some form of nastiness. Rumors of affairs and other repugnant behavior is unfortunately part of the campaign season. But what has changed in my lifetime is that those rumors have become more pervasive because of how easy they are to spread. It is no revelation that Christians are guilty of this, especially during the election cycle, as they claim to support the only

---

14. González and Jiménez, *Púlpito*, 26.

qualified person for the job and their opponent is a traitorous villain. As someone who loves history, I enjoy election season. But as a pastor, I loathe it. It brings out the worst in otherwise pleasant people.

I've thought a lot about how this has come to be accepted by those in the church. The only answer I can come up with is that many of us have forgotten how to love one another. We love through acts of service and selflessness. We give of our time, energy, and finances so that others will be blessed. We also give by valuing and honoring one another, even if means that we face discomfort and difficulty. We do those things because God first loved us, so loving becomes second nature to us.

But this kind of sacrificial commitment to love through our preaching can quickly become thwarted by our own desire for territory. We have *our* style of preaching. We have *our* convictions. Our aim as believers is to value and serve the other *above* our own desires and preferences. Schultze notes:

> Identification equips us to learn to speak others' languages, to interpret their gestures, and to understand their images ... Christ touched the lepers and spoke with the prostitutes and tax-collectors. He communed with all types of people in all types of social classes regardless of their standing in the religious community. As God's image bearers we share some of that ability to identify with others every time we communicate ... entering into a people's conversations and stories ... God's grace enables us to let go of our immediate assumptions and pre-conceptions so that we can identify with others. We no longer merely observe others, we begin to participate with them.[15]

Loving someone—especially those who don't share our story—requires that we work to identify blind spots in our thinking and preaching so that we can help others come to love the gospel.

Practices to Help Preachers Grow Their Cultural Intelligence

Though this section will not be exhaustive, I think there are some practical things preachers can do to improve their cultural intelligence. The most basic recommendation would be to spend time studying the community in which you live. Know the neighborhoods and the demographics. Read as much as you can about the community and talk with residents, especially

15. Schultze, *Communicating for Life*, 35–36.

those who have lived there a long time. You will see why certain neighborhoods are predominately one race or ethnicity and how things have changed over time.[16] Eating at local restaurants, particularly those owned and frequented by those with different backgrounds and ethnicities, is an exceptional way to get to know people.

We need to spend time with people who don't fit into the majority groups. What I have often heard from brothers and sister of a different ethnicity is that they haven't had many white folks actually listen to them. Everyone has a story and knowing these will certainly have an impact in how we craft our sermons. One mistake that I have made more times than I'm proud to admit is that I went into these conversations with the best intentions, only to find myself pushing back and arguing whenever something was said that didn't fit into what I believed to be right. We need to ask questions and listen to what people have to say. This certainly applies to everyone; it's a sign of being a superb listener who is interested in others, but it's especially true when listening to people who, historically, have not been heard.

We need to listen to preachers of different ethnicities and backgrounds. It is so much easier and more enjoyable to find preachers who fit our theology and preferred preaching style, but that's not the way we grow. We grow by being challenged and engaging with new ideas. This goes against the political culture in the United States where, if someone disagrees with you, it makes them an enemy. Proverbs 15:1 says, "A soft answer turns away wrath, but a harsh word stirs up anger." Most translations use the term gentle, but the meaning is the same. A mark of Christian maturity is the ability to lovingly engage with different ideas and have the other person leave feeling heard, valued, and cared for. That should be our goal for our preaching as well.[17]

---

16. Two books that I recommend to everyone at this stage are *The Color of Law: A Forgotten History of How Our Government Segregated America* by Richard Rothstein (2018) and *The Color of Compromise: The Truth About the American Church's Complicity in Racism* by Jemar Tisby (2019).

17. Two books that deal with this are *A Gentle Answer: Our 'Secret Weapon' in an Age of Us Against Them* by Scott Sauls (2020) and *Republocrat: Confessions of a Liberal Conservative* by Carl Trueman (2010).

Conclusion

Everything in this chapter should bring us back to our primary calling; to show how the gospel is the answer to the problem that we face: our own sin and how our sin has separated us from the holiness of God. Some cultures understand the idea of sin as law breaking. Other cultures focus on shame. Still others see the gospel in terms of a familial restoration. There is one gospel but there are many ways to explain and apply it.

I'm afraid that too many of us (myself included, unfortunately) have come to believe that there is only one way to share the gospel or there is only one way to preach. Our cultural norms and experiences have brought us to this point and many of us have run with that. Our preaching has been successful with a certain demographic, but we have not been able to connect well with people who don't come from the same background or ethnicity as our own. In the next chapter, we will look at how the gospel changes everything for us.

The good news is that conflict in the church is often followed by great efforts to restore unity. In his book, *Divided We Fall: Overcoming a History of Christian Disunity*, Luder Whitlock holds that diversity in the church "can easily spawn misunderstanding and tensions that escalate into anger, hostility, and division, especially when confronted with adversity or sudden change." For Whitlock, church history has proven this. He writes:

> From its inception, the church has never achieved more than an imperfect experience of its unity in Christ. Various problems and divisions have seemingly been perpetual. This has been painful and disappointing, but it is a reality that must be acknowledged. Yet it may also be argued that many of these conflicts were matched by equally endless and sincere—and sometimes sacrificial—efforts to restore unity.[18]

This is certainly good news! What I hope this chapter has done is cause you to think through how you can incorporate best practices of intercultural communication into your preaching, particularly thinking about what conflicts could arise and address those before they begin in your preaching.

David Livermore notes that the primary benefit for us to have a multicultural/multi-ethnic church is that the gospel becomes clearer. He notes:

> There's something secure and stabilizing about being with people who view the world like us. Laughing together about things we find

---

18. Whitlock Jr., *Divided We Fall*, 13.

funny, ranting together about things that tick us off and sharing an appreciation for some of the same food, art, and perspectives on the world can be the ingredients for building serendipitous memories together. But quite honestly, there's nothing very remarkable about enjoying time with people like ourselves. Everyone fares pretty well there. But to love and appreciate someone who despises the very things we value and vice versa—now that's another story. Yet the real mystery of the gospel lies in how we deal with those relationships of difference.[19]

This gospel mystery will be unfolded in detail in the next chapter. Here, we see that having a keen cultural awareness allows us to be the church—people from different backgrounds, ethnicities, and cultures, who can come together for one common purpose.

---

19. Livermore, *Cultural Intelligence*, 18.

4

How the Gospel Changes Everything

THUS FAR I HAVE briefly taken a long-range view of the biblical and cultural demand for preachers to know their audience and deliver sermons in a way that resonates with as many people as possible. This means preachers will need to study their community in addition to studying God's Word. But what is the point in all of this? Is it to make the community a better or a safer place to live? Is it to help people out of poverty? Is it to give every child three meals a day? That is certainly the primary mission of some churches, but it misunderstands and misapplies the biblical narrative. The gospel is the reason for everything we do. In this chapter, I will discuss the gospel with a focus on how the biblical is different from the social gospel. From there, I will show how the gospel impacts every aspect of our lives, including issues of race and ethnicity. In other words, social justice is not part of the gospel but it is an effect of the gospel.

What is the Gospel?

So, what is the gospel? In truth, the first three chapters assume that the reader understands what I mean when I use the term *gospel*. But to someone new to the faith, or perhaps someone who isn't part of the Christian faith, the term gospel could mean a variety of things. It could mean a style of music, either soulful music from the tradition of the African-American church or it could mean music that we hear in southern tent revivals. For others, the word gospel has no real meaning at all—something people have heard but can't really tell you what it means.

According to DeYoung, et al., liberation theology teaches that the gospel changes for different groups and situations, but ultimately, "the gospel must be liberated from dominant group interpretations." DeYoung, et al., write that in the United States, the gospel of liberation theology primarily addresses things like "racism, economic exploitation, discrimination, and ethnocentrism."[1] What I don't want any reader to think is that the gospel doesn't touch on those things. It certainly does and we will deal with that in more detail in chapter 7, but liberation theology (and others like it) make an effect of the gospel the gospel itself. Let me give an illustration to help explain what I mean: I am the father of my children. There is nothing that my kids can do to change that fact. But simply being their father doesn't mean that I love them. Anyone can love my kids, but that doesn't mean the sweet old man at church who hugs my kids each week becomes their father. The love that I have for them is an effect of me being their father, not the other way around.

The reason the supposed gospel of liberation theology falls apart is that it focuses on making the world a better place. It takes an effect of the gospel and turns it into the substance of the gospel, similar to my illustration where simply loving my kids does not make someone their father. Liberation theology does not and cannot answer our biggest problem: that our sin has separated us from God. That is the beginning of the true gospel. Jerry Bridges puts it this way: "It is the good news that directly addresses the ultimate bad news of our lives. The Bible tells us that we were in deep trouble with God, that we were unrighteous and ungodly. And then it tells us that God's wrath is revealed from heaven 'against all the godlessness and wickedness of men.'"[2]

Pastor Greg Gilbert, in his book *What is the Gospel?*, uses Romans 1–4 as a path for what the gospel is. First, in Romans 1, Paul tells the reader that they are accountable to God. In Rom1:18, Paul says, "For the wrath of God is revealed from heaven against all ungodliness and unrighteousness of men, who by their unrighteousness suppress the truth." This is our diagnosis. A good doctor would not look at the results of an MRI and then proceed to discuss the cure without any discussion of the condition; a good

---

1. DeYoung et al., *United by Faith*, 117.
2. Bridges, *Gospel for Real Life*, 17.

doctor will explain what the MRI says before giving the solution to the problem. The bad news always comes before the good news, otherwise the good news will make no sense.

Second, Paul tells the reader that the problem everyone must deal with is that they have rebelled against God. Romans 1:22–23 says, "Claiming to be wise, they became fools, and exchanged the glory of the immortal God for images resembling mortal man and birds and animals and creeping things." This description of our condition continues through the end of chapter 1 and into chapter 2:

> They were filled with all manner of unrighteousness, evil, covetousness, malice. They are full of envy, murder, strife, deceit, maliciousness. They are gossips, slanderers, haters of God, insolent, haughty, boastful, inventors of evil, disobedient to parents, foolish, faithless, heartless, ruthless. Though they know God's righteous decree that those who practice such things deserve to die, they not only do them but give approval to those who practice them. Therefore you have no excuse.

Because of our willful rebellion, we have no excuse before God. Our sin has made us guilty. The only right punishment for our rebellion is death. Paul says in Rom 3:23, "For all have sinned and fall short of the glory of God." Since God cannot allow sin to achieve any victory, the guilty verdict that we earned demands justice. Based on the human system of justice and our own views of fair punishment, we would not sentence someone to eternal punishment. Our idea of fairness prevents us from seeing the wretchedness of our own sin. James 2:10 says, "For whoever keeps the whole law but fails in one point has become guilty of it." One sin is the same as committing endless sin.

Our guilt is not just from our actions but who we do it against. If someone threatens to kill a bug, no one is going to complain. But if that same person threatens to kill their neighbor, there is a problem. Now, suppose that person threatens to kill the President of the United States. The crime is the same, but the punishment will be tremendously different based on whom the threat was made against. If someone sins against me, they will only feel the temporary sting of whatever I can give. But sinning against God is altogether different. He is the lawgiver. He is the one who deserves and demands perfection from his creation.

The gospel tells us that there is no way that we can accomplish perfection on our own. No matter how much good we do or how many people we help or how much money we give away, there is nothing that we can do that will make us right in the eyes of God. Sure, people will see our philanthropy and all of the sacrifices we have made for others, but God sees the filth and rebellion that reside in our hearts. So, our sin prevents us from saving ourselves. We are hopeless and helpless. We are dead.

This brings us to Gilbert's third point: Paul says that the solution to our problem is the sacrificial death and resurrection of Jesus. Romans 3:22–24 says, "the righteousness of God through faith in Jesus Christ for all who believe. For there is no distinction: for all have sinned and fall short of the glory of God, and are justified by his grace as a gift, through the redemption that is in Christ Jesus." Romans 5:8 says, "God shows his love for us in that while we were still sinners, Christ died for us." Jesus lived a perfect life so that we could have his righteousness credited to our account. He died on the cross so that he could take the wrath of God that we deserve.

Finally, Paul tells the reader how they can be included in this salvation. Paul says in Rom 3:22 that salvation belongs to all who believe.[3] Bridges argues, "We owe an enormous spiritual debt to God—a debt that we can't begin to pay. There is no way we can make it good. The gospel tells us that Jesus Christ paid our debt, but it also tells us far more. It tells us that we are no longer enemies and objects of His wrath. We are now His sons and daughters, heirs with Jesus Christ . . ."[4] That is the gospel.

In Genesis 1 God created the world and it was good. In chapter 2 of this study, we saw how everyone has inherent worth because every human being was created in the image of God. Nothing else in the universe has this distinction, but it didn't take long for the first two humans to ignore this. Adam's sin—his desire to be like God—changed his relationship with God forever, as it did for everyone after him. Humanity owed a debt that none of us could repay. We couldn't be holy enough to make God happy with us but God's plan all along was that the only one who is—Jesus—would take our place in enduring the wrath of God. I recognize that I am repeating what I just said a few paragraphs ago, but I do that for a purpose: this is the most important thing any preacher can give to his audience. No amount of memorable sermons, catchy phrases, or vivid illustrations can compare to the wonderful, yet simple, gospel message. It often does not draw a crowd, but it does bring glory to the Savior.

3. Gilbert, *Gospel?*, 28–31.
4. Bridges, *Gospel for Real Life*, 19.

This is what it means to be gospel-centered. To have the gospel at the center of everything we say and do is our calling. It is our nutrition. It sustains us. It gives us energy and vitality. But, let's be honest, the term gospel-centered has become too trendy: gospel-centered preaching, gospel-centered discipleship, and gospel-centered counseling. With everything so gospel-centered, has the term lost its meaning? I'm sure that, somewhere, there are businesses who pride themselves in being gospel-centered storage facilities or gospel-centered sandwich shops, but that doesn't mean that Christians should avoid using it or, at least, it doesn't mean that Christians should avoid the concept. The gospel should color everything we do. To selfishly massacre a famous line from Abraham Kuyper: there is not one square inch of our existence that fails to be impacted by the gospel.[5] I am limited in my oratory skills and I'm certainly not brilliant by any stretch, but I do know what Jesus has done for me. I may not always have the right words to describe deep, theological concepts, but I can tell you the solution to the biggest problem you have. You, brother, must be like the Apostle Paul: decide "to know nothing . . . except Jesus Christ and him crucified."

There is a quote that has been attributed to Nicolaus Zinzendorf, a leader in the Moravian church in the eighteenth century: "Preach the gospel, die, be forgotten." I've probably used this quote a few dozen times in my preaching because it is what I want for my ministry. John the Baptist said about Jesus, "He must increase, but I must decrease." Our calling is to preach the gospel, it is not to ourselves. This is what I mean—and I think it's what others mean—when I talk about being gospel-centered. The only thing of value that we can offer our people is a life that has been changed by the gospel and that is devoted to telling people how they can receive the same gift.

The Need for Contextualization

This sounds so simple, doesn't it? Just preach the gospel and God will be glorified. That is what I often hear at conferences, and I while I agree that there is only one gospel, how it's presented is often vastly different across cultures. In his book, *Free at Last? The Gospel in the African-American*

---

5. The full quote is: "Oh, no single piece of our mental world is to be hermetically sealed off from the rest, and there is not a square inch in the whole domain of our human existence over which Christ, who is Sovereign over all, does not cry: 'Mine!'" See Bratt, *Abraham Kuyper*, 488.

Experience, Carl Ellis details a painful history of Christianity for black Americans. He notes that there is an emphasis in white evangelicalism that focuses on the individual experience, making one's faith more about "me and God" than God and his people. In discussing why so many white evangelicals failed to take a strong stand during the Civil Rights movement in the United States, he charges:

> Sadly, many White evangelical, fundamentalist, and Reformed churches were caught sleeping with no oil in their lamps at the outbreak of this move of God in the land. They had evidently been rendered dysfunctional by a defective view of theology and culture. They failed to distinguish between White standards and scriptural standards. Their theology had led them to a preoccupation with private salvation.
>
> The importance of personal salvation should never be diminished. But the whole counsel of God revealed in the Scriptures goes far beyond the scope of the private realm. According to God's Word, even salvation itself finds its significance in terms of a much larger picture—namely, the praise of God's glory (Ephesians 1–2). But many leading evangelicals never came to grips with the big picture of God's purposes. They never saw the broad cultural implications of the Great Commission. This is why their Christianity never had application beyond the private aspects of life. Many believed that America's racial injustices would fade away automatically as more individuals had conversion experiences. This naïve view completely ignored the patterns of racism that had been woven into the American system.[6]

Ellis believes that so many black Christians sided with more liberal pastors and theologians because the liberal pastors and theologians sided with them first. Ellis thinks that this is one of the primary reasons the gospel sounds so different in most white churches compared to most black churches.

Scholar Anthony Bradley has an alternate explanation for the gospel sounding different. In a series of posts on Twitter, Bradley explained that the root of the differences lies in who people get to Jesus through:

> Generally in the black church, you learn about Jesus through Moses. Evangelicals, Paul. That's why evangelicals struggle w/social issues. When you get to Jesus through Moses, redemption encompasses all of life. God is redeeming the whole creation. People, places, & things. When you get to Jesus through Paul ("the gospel")

6. Ellis, Jr., *Free at Last?*, 81–82.

redemption is becomes largely about issues of personal salvation & the church. The Pauline starting point has to do some hermeneutical gymnastics to make a case for how the gospel applies to X because of Paul's scope. Alternatively, the Mosaic starting point is free to articulate why God cares abt [sic] personal salvation, economics, business, education, etc. Therefore the black church tradition, had an easier time making a case for why God cared abt [sic] slavery, Jim Crow, civil-rights, etc. The black church tradition, generally did not have to defend Christian witness in society light of the contextual priorities of Paul. As a result, modern evangelical systematic theology books (like Grudem et al) are categorically deficient for racial minorities. Leaders of ethnic minorities need systematic theologies w/the priorities of Moses *and* Paul which culminate in the work/person of Christ. I now understand why I never really "got" the evangelical insistence that Xianity reflect Paul's priorities. I wasn't raised that way. This is what black liberation theology was attempting to do: provide a non-dominant culture (mainly Pauline) witness of Christ. For the 21st century, African, black, Latin/o orthodox Xian [sic] pastors/theologians need collaboration b/c evangelical sources are deficient. Black, African, Latin/o Christians need to do more than regurgitate/parrot the theological priorities (& blindspots) of white evangelism. Finally, Black, African, Latin/o Christian still need their own movement instead of the dominant one decorated with minority ornaments.[7]

Kenyatta Gilbert, echoing what we see in liberation theology, explains, "Blacks did not use Christianity as whites first introduced it to them without making certain substantial changes that took into consideration their oppressive condition and other contextual factors."[8] In conversations with black pastors, I have heard a few mention that they see the gospel through the eyes of the minor prophets. One person mentioned that the minor prophets are valuable in understanding the gospel because they wrote in a time that was far removed from the miracles of the older books, most notably the Pentateuch.

In some of the examples listed above the pastors largely agree on the gospel. Ellis, Bradley, and the men I've spoken with over the years would all agree that they are reformed in their understanding of God's sovereignty in salvation. Yet, they see the gospel through different lenses. The challenge to a preacher comes in how to communicate with the congregation, even

---

7. Bradley, "Black Church, Moses and Evangelical Church," Twitter, January 3, 2017.
8. Gilbert, *Journey and Promise of African American Preaching*, 34.

when folks from the same socio-economic and ethnic backgrounds see things from different angles.

This section has focused, up to this point, solely on how African-Americans see the gospel. Things get increasingly difficult when many other ethnicities and backgrounds are brought into a local church. Professor Soong-Chan Rah at North Park Theological Seminary in Chicago notes, "Most Christians understand the terms *gospel* or *good news*. However, there are subtle, nuanced differences in how even the most astute Christian may perceive the concept of good news." He gives the following examples to help describe this in more detail:

> In the Greco-Roman context, which tends to be the only context and lens through which we read the New Testament, the Greek word for "gospel" (*euangelion*) is the declaration that a son has been born to the emperor, the good news being that the line of the succession would continue with the birth of the male offspring. A herald was sent forth to proclaim this good news, evocative of the heavenly hosts proclaiming the joyful news to the shepherds of the birth of the Son of God. The gospel is the proclamation of this good news.
>
> In the Hebrew context, the word for "gospel" focuses more on the presence of YHWH and His kingdom. For example, in Isaiah 52:7, we see the declaration of the good news. The passage (paraphrased) proclaims: "How lovely on the mountains are the feet of him who brings *good news*. Announcing peace and proclaiming the news of happiness, that *Our God Reigns*." Good news in the Hebrew context means the reign of God is here. The exiles are encouraged by the promise that God reigns and His rule will be demonstrated among His people. The focus of the good news in Isaiah is not only the proclamation, but also the demonstration of the good news. God's reign should not only be talked about, but lived out and lived into.
>
> In the twenty-first century, we can look back at the two seemingly disparate definitions of good news and fail to see the intersection and synergy between the two concepts. While potentially differing cultural values and paradigms may be at work, we can hope that the intersection of these two cultures will produce a fuller version than what has gone before.
>
> The gospel, therefore, is not merely the proclamation of the good news. It is not simply going door to door and telling people that Jesus loves them. The gospel is incomplete if it is reduced to simple proclamation.

> At the same time, the gospel is not simply living into the good news (i.e., the demonstration of salvation). Not only must the reign of God be demonstrated, it must also be proclaimed. Both the Greco-Roman perspective on the good news and the Hebrew perspective on the good news work together to provide a fuller meaning of the gospel.[9]

What Rah shows, particularly in the last paragraph of the above quote, is that the preacher must be able to present truth in a variety of ways in order to better communicate the gospel to his listeners. What this means is that the preacher has much to consider when creating and delivering his sermons. It is not that the redemptive gospel has changed. What is different is the way we hear, interpret, and connect the gospel to our lives.

Though we will go deeper into contextualization in chapter 7, it's important to recognize it here because it is necessary in our presentation of the gospel. Ed Stetzer defines contextualization as "presenting the gospel in culturally relevant ways." He contends, "Contextualization is an important component of effective Gospel ministry. The Gospel is an eternal, transcultural reality, but it comes to us within the context of a human culture. Contemporary Christians should carefully seek to discern the difference between Gospel truth and cultural tradition."[10] In other words, contextualization is taking something from Scripture and explaining it using words that are familiar to the listener.

I knew a preacher whose sermons would often sound more like religious lectures. His intentions were noble; he wanted the church to grow in their knowledge of the Scripture, so he would preach for well over an hour. Many grew tired of these long sermons because there are few preachers who can keep an audience's attention for that long. This preacher would regularly call people goats (as opposed to sheep) and he would complain that people who left the church couldn't take the hard preaching he would deliver each week. In reality, he was mostly preaching to himself. He was far too academic for most people and it caused countless problems for his ministry because he could never understand why few people appreciated his sermons, even though they were full of doctrine and truth. Tim Keller addresses this: "It is possible to merely assert and confront and feel we have been very "valiant for truth," but if you are dry or tedious, people will not repent and believe the

---

9. Rah, *Many Colors*, 109–10.

10. Ed Stetzer, "What Is Contextualization? Presenting the Gospel in Culturally Relevant Ways."

right doctrine you present. We must preach so that, as in the first sermon on Pentecost, hearers are "cut to the heart" (Acts 2:37)."[11]

According to Pastor Manuel Ortiz, contextualization is a necessity if the gospel is to make sense to anyone. He argues,

> The church must keep in mind that linguistics is only one cultural criterion. A youthful population that is trying to determine its identity and destiny will need sensitive Christians to assist it. In the process, the church will be challenged in its cultural traditions, its theological perspective and its ecclesiastical formation. It must wrestle deeply with the issues of contextualization. Theology's ability to transform all of life will be tested. When the church believes it is to be soul centered, its only responsibility will be challenged. The gospel will be relevant when it becomes the good news for all of life, for the totality of the people's historical situation.[12]

This should come as no surprise because we already accept this as true in our normal communication. When I describe something that happened in sports to someone who doesn't follow sports, I must contextualize what I'm saying so that what I'm saying makes sense. The quickest way for a preacher to lose the attention of his audience is to use words and terms that mean nothing to those listening. David Livermore observes, "The good news can become the good news to oppressed and broken people only if it is translated into pictures and experiences they can understand."[13] For Livermore, having cultural intelligence—which he defines as "the ability to move seamlessly in and out of a variety of cultural contexts"—is essential if we are to simply be understood.[14]

Social Justice and the Gospel

A significant part of the problem that pastors have in the area of cultural intelligence comes from the fact that, often, the preacher and listener actually speak the same language. The confusion is easy to spot if an English-speaking preacher stands in front of a room of Spanish speaking individuals. Without a translator, what the preacher says will be complete gibberish to the audience. That's an obvious situation where communication fails. But what about

11. Keller, *Preaching*, 157.
12. Ortiz, *Hispanic Challenge*, 39.
13. Livermore, *Cultural Intelligence*, 33.
14. Livermore, *Cultural Intelligence*, 47.

when the preacher is a native English speaker and the audience is primarily Spanish speakers who know enough English to make sense of most of what the preacher is saying? This confusion can be addressed through avoiding idioms and culturally specific language. Sure, it takes work, but much of the confusion between speaker and listener can be avoided.

But what happens when the preacher and listeners speak the same language and even use the same words, but have different meanings for the words being spoken? For the last few years, the discussion of racism seems to have reached a boiling point. What I have seen has bothered me a great deal because I see men who stand side-by-side on the gospel and who even preach at each other's churches, yet they seem to be separating from one another over racism. To be fair, it's not the idea of racism. Most everyone will say that racism is bad, but how exactly are they defining the term? This is what Emerson and Smith found in their book *Divided by Faith*. They interviewed white evangelicals and black evangelicals, asking each person the same list of questions. What they found was that whites and blacks, in large part, have a very different understanding of not only what racism was but also what to do about it. They write:

> ... white evangelicals place strong emphasis on family relationships, friendships, church relationships, and other forms of interpersonal connections. Healthy relationships encourage people to make right choices. For this reason, white evangelicals, as we see, often view social problems as rooted in poor relationships or the negative influence of significant others.
> ... For most white evangelicals ... sin is limited to individuals. Thus, if race problems—poor relationships—result from sin, then race problems must largely be individually based.[15]

In other words, most white Christians will admit that racism is real, but they see it as an individual problem, one that can only be fixed by people getting to know and loving one another.

What Emerson and Smith discovered was that when most white Christians talk about racism, it is almost always in terms of one-on-one relationships. The authors write, "The white evangelicals we interviewed do not want a race problem. They want to see people get along, and want people to have equal opportunity. They see these as essential to living out their faith. In short, they yearn for color-blind people. This is the contemporary

---

15. Emerson and Smith, *Divided By Faith*, 77–78.

white American evangelical perspective."[16] White and black folks will stand together to denounce racism—as long as it's visible, undeniable, and done by an individual or individuals. But the discussion turns a different direction when black Christians mention systemic racism. Shouts from the white crowd ring out: "Show me the exact moment of racism and then I'll believe you." Their intentions are good, but the black Christians are hurt because what they have experienced has been reduced to figments of their collective imaginations.

Emerson and Smith illustrate this point often in their study. They say that the problem is not just between individuals. It exists much deeper than that, in society as a whole, as well as the systems that serve as the structure for everyday life. They write that the average white American evangelical perspective misses the patterns that transcend individuals. It is in these— the often hidden or beneath the surface forces at work—where the enduring problems are. They write:

> It misses that whites can move to most any neighborhood, eat at most any restaurant, walk down most any street, or shop at most any store without having to worry or find out that they are not wanted, whereas African Americans often cannot. This perspective misses that white Americans can be almost certain that when stopped by the police, it has nothing to do with race, whereas African Americans cannot. This perspective misses that whites are assumed to be middle class unless proven otherwise, are not expected to speak for their race, can remain ignorant of other cultures without penalty, and do not have to ask every time something goes wrong if it is due to race, whereas African Americans cannot. This perspective misses that white Americans are far more likely than black Americans to get a solid education, avoid being the victim of a crime, and have family and friends with money to help when extra cash is needed for college, a car, or a house. This perspective misses that white Americans are far more likely to have networks and connections that lead to good jobs than are black Americans. This perspective misses that white Americans are far more likely to get fair treatment in the court system than are African Americans.[17]

The list Emerson and Smith give is not exhaustive, but it is a brief glimpse into the differences that white Americans rarely see. The first time

---

16. Emerson and Smith, *Divided By Faith*, 89.
17. Emerson and Smith, *Divided By Faith*, 90.

I read *Divided by Faith*, I remember having to put the book down every few pages because what I was seeing on the page was so new and disturbing. I never considered that racism was anything more than someone not liking someone because of their skin color. Not once did I examine the world as it must be for a person of color in the United States.

There is a danger that our gospel-centered preaching can quickly become man-centered if we shift focus from the gospel to issues of social justice. A few pages ago, I mentioned that I have been bothered by pastors who agree on almost everything break fellowship over issues of race and justice. One side says that this is nothing more than Marxism with a Christian veneer. But is that true? It certainly can be. Individuals have forsaken the gospel in favor of fixing the ills of this world here and now, but that's not what everyone is doing. There are men from theologically conservative and Reformed perspectives who don't see social justice as the gospel. They see the gospel leading them to work for justice here and now. They see injustices like the list from Emerson and Smith and they ask, "How does the gospel address this?" They ask, "What good is it if someone says he has faith but does not have works?" The gospel is what matters most and it is that same gospel that propels these brothers to address issues of injustice from the pulpit.

What I have learned is that the gospel touches every aspect of my life as a Christian. I hope that every Christian would condemn racial slurs, but what do we do when we see black men make up 6 percent of the US adult population but are approximately 35 percent of the prison population? What do we do when we see that blacks receive much longer prison sentences than whites for the same crime?[18] Do we stay silent? Unfortunately, many preachers have spoken up but not in support of our black brothers and sisters. It does not take much searching to find white preachers who are more concerned with proving how wrong someone's feelings are, than they are about bandaging up their wounds.

Though racism and systemic injustice have always been present, as have the calls to fix those things that are broken, the public outcry and demands for action reached a boiling point in 2012 with the shooting of Trayvon Martin. Michael Brown in Ferguson, MO, Eric Garner in New York, and others would follow, each providing examples of problems that African Americans deal with in the United States. For many white Americans, these were isolated issues that can be answered with a string of facts

---

18. Starr and Rehavi, "Racial Disparity in Federal Criminal Sentences," 1320–54.

and logical argumentation. The problem with this, from a Christian and pastoral perspective, is that millions of people were telling us that they were hurting and the only response they could hear was, "You have no reason to be hurting." Whether that is what we are saying or not, that is what so many African Americans hear and that is a problem, especially when it comes from the pulpit. Our voice must be one of compassion and care, not arguing and justification.

Racism in any form won't be cured from the pulpit, but that doesn't mean we can neglect it. The history of black Americans being abused, mistreated, and unfairly looked at by the dominant white establishment is long and people in our community need to hear that they have a friend and an advocate in their pastor. I serve in the Southern Baptist Convention (SBC), which has a sad history in the area of civil rights and compassion. Russell Moore, the former president of the Ethics & Religious Liberty Commission of the SBC, has been an outspoken advocate for racial justice. He argues:

> My denomination was founded back in the nineteenth century by those who advocated for human slavery, and who sought to keep their consciences and their ballots and their wallets away from a transcendent word that would speak against the sinful injustice of a regime of kidnapping, rape, and human beings wickedly deigning to buy and sell other human beings created in the image of God. Slavery, they argued (to their shame), was a "political" issue that ought not distract the church from its mission: evangelism and discipleship. What such a move empowered was not just social injustice (which would have been bad enough), but also personal sin. When so-called "simple gospel preaching" churches in 1856 Alabama or 1925 Mississippi calls sinners to repentance for fornicating and gambling but not for slaveholding or lynching, those churches may be many things but they are hardly non-political. By not addressing these issues, they are addressing them, by implicitly stating that they are not worthy of the moral scrutiny of the church, that they will not be items of report at the Judgment Seat of Christ. These churches, thus, bless the status quo, with all the fealty of a court chaplain. The same is true of a church in twenty-first-century America that doesn't speak to the pressing issues of justice and righteousness around us, such as the horror of abortion and the persisting sins of racial injustice.[19]

---

19. Moore, *Onward*, 99.

Silence from the pulpit speaks volumes to those who come to us hurting with the trauma they have experienced as both individuals and as people with a shared history and memory.

What we've seen over the last few years is a strong push-back from some against anyone who does not see how an obedience to Christ and a love for the gospel and our neighbor pushes believers to work for justice. A statement signed by John MacArthur, James White, Voddie Baucham, and over thirteen thousand others, has many honorable qualities: they affirm the gospel and that every human being is an image bearer. This statement, however, denies the existence of systemic racism:

> We deny that Christians should segregate themselves into racial groups or regard racial identity above, or even equal to, their identity in Christ. We deny that any divisions between people groups (from an unstated attitude of superiority to an overt spirit of resentment) have any legitimate place in the fellowship of the redeemed. We reject any teaching that encourages racial groups to view themselves as privileged oppressors or entitled victims of oppression. While we are to weep with those who weep, we deny that a person's feelings of offense or oppression necessarily prove that someone else is guilty of sinful behaviors, oppression, or prejudice.[20]

While the statement about weeping with those who weep is helpful and seems to come from a genuine place of pastoral care, the rest of the statement is often received as cold.

This statement was published as a response to two conferences where the racism was addressed. The first conference, held April 3–4, 2018 in Memphis, TN was called "MLK50: Gospel Reflections from the Mountaintop." It was joint-sponsored by Russell Moore's Ethics & Religious Liberty Commission (SBC) and The Gospel Coalition. This conference addressed how the vision of Dr. Martin Luther King, Jr. still holds today and how the gospel is the only thing that answers the problem of racism. Some well-known preachers and pastors spoke at this conference: John Piper, H.B. Charles, Eric Mason, Matt Chandler, and John Perkins, to name just a few.

The social media frenzy was multiplied when, just one week later in Louisville, Kentucky, David Platt spoke at the biennial Together for the Gospel conference. Christians on social media, aided by discernment blogs, criticized Platt's sermon as not being a true expositional sermon.[21]

---

20. "The Statement on Social Justice & the Gospel."
21. Platt, "Let Justice Roll Down Like Waters: Racism and Our Need for Repentance."

His text was Amos 5:18–27, which did not directly address issues of race, though Platt showed how the text of Scripture speaks to issues that plague our modern culture. Part of the uproar Platt faced after his sermon was that he didn't spend enough time on the explanation of the passage. The first six minutes of the sermon was an introduction where he asked for grace from the audience, and an explanation of how he had failed to live up to what he was proclaiming. The next eight minutes fit in well with the definition of expository preaching that we saw in chapter 1. Platt explained the context of the passage as well as how God was using Amos.

As a bridge from the introduction, Platt outlined three primary offenses that Amos addressed. First, from verses 18–20, "They were eagerly anticipating future salvation while they were conveniently denying present sin." In other words, the people were willfully denying their sin while waiting for their own salvation. Second, from verses 21–26, "they were indulging in worship while they were ignoring injustice." Third, from verses 25–27, "they were carrying on their religion while they were refusing to repent." Platt stated, "Our God is not honored by mouths that are quick to sing and hands that are quick to rise in worship, when those same mouths are slow to speak and those same hands are slow to work against injustice. Our God hates worship like that." And as his bridge to application: "have we been or are we now slow to speak and work against racial injustice around us?" In the application, Platt gave six exhortations: look at the reality of racism; live in true multi-ethnic community; listen to and learn from one another; love and lay aside our preferences for one another; leverage our influence for justice in the present; and long for the day when justice will be perfect. This sermon was heavy on application, but it was also heavy on the gospel. In multiple instances, Platt explained what the gospel is and why and how the gospel answers racism.

There is no requirement for an expositional sermon to have a certain percentage of detailed historical analysis and explanation of the text in comparison to application. Some passages require less explanation of the situation of the text and far more application for something that is happening in the world and needs to be addressed. After any tragedy, pastors all over the country will bring a message of encouragement from Scripture that is heavier on application than their normal preaching. This is what Platt was doing in his sermon.

John Stott wrote that the preacher's job is to build a bridge from the ancient text to today. A large part of that for the expositor is showing how the Bible is relevant to the lives of the people and that, in large part, comes through application of the text. Stott attests that every generation has had questions they want answered:

> What is the purpose of our existence? Has life any significance? Where did I come from, and where am I going to? What does it mean to be a human being, and how do humans differ from animals? Whence this thirst for transcendence, this universal quest for a Reality above and beyond us, this need to fall down and worship the Infinitely Great? What is freedom, and how can I experience personal liberation? Why the painful tension between what I am and what I long to be? Is there a way to be rid of guilt and of a guilty conscience? What about the hunger for love, sexual fulfillment, marriage, family life and community on the one hand, and on the other the pervasive sense of alienation, and the base, destructive passions of jealousy, malice, hate, lust and revenge? Is it possible truly to master oneself and love one's neighbour? Is there any light on the dark mysteries of evil and suffering? How can we find courage to face first life, then death, then what may lie beyond death? What hope can sustain us in the midst of our despair?
>
> In every generation and every culture men and women have asked these questions and debated these issues. This is the stuff from which the world's great literature is formed. Have we Christians nothing to say about these things? Of course we have! We are convinced that the questions themselves reflect and bear witness to the paradoxical nature of human beings which the Bible teaches, namely their dignity as Godlike creatures and their depravity as fallen and guilty sinners. We are also convinced that Jesus Christ either has the answers to these questions or—in the case of intractable mysteries like pain and evil—that he throws more light on them than can be gathered from any other source. Jesus Christ, we believe, is the fulfillment of every truly human aspiration. To find him is to find ourselves.[22]

Though Stott doesn't include issues of race and ethnicity, those things would have been on his list had he written that in 2020. Later in the same book, Stott gives his thoughts on what the task of the preacher is:

> Our task as preachers, then, is neither to avoid all areas of controversy, nor to supply slick answers to complex questions in order to save people the bother of thinking. Either way is to treat them like children who are unable to think for themselves, and to condemn

---

22. Stott, *Between Two Worlds*, 151.

them to perpetual immaturity. Instead, it is our responsibility to teach them with clarity and conviction the plain truths of Scripture, in order to help them develop a Christian mind, and to encourage them to think with it about the great problems of the day, and so to grow into maturity in Christ.[23]

It may be unpopular in some circles to deal with issues of justice, but our task is not to avoid all areas of controversy. We are to show what the Bible says, how the gospel addresses issues of our day, and what we as Christians must do to live in obedience.

I think the "Statement on Social Justice & the Gospel" echoes what many white evangelicals feel today. They aren't racist as individuals, but so many of our black brothers and sisters have expressed that silence from white Christians or even pushback to what they have experienced supports the racist systems and structures that have been so harmful to so many.

A Word of Warning

I would be remiss if I didn't include a warning for the preacher. As with most of life, we must seek out balance in how we live, think, and communicate. When dealing with complex and nuanced issues of race and ethnicity, history, and what to do going forward, there is a danger of going too far. As previously stated, "The Statement on Social Justice & the Gospel" correctly emphasizes the gospel as the main priority for Christians, but it does so at the expense of addressing societal ills. The correct elevation of the gospel should not mean that other important issues are ignored, downplayed, or argued against.

Likewise, there is a danger of going to the extreme on the other side. This is what MacArthur and the others were warning against in their statement. The most obvious danger is that social issues become elevated to the point that social justice is the focus instead of the gospel. Paul tells Timothy in 1 Tim 6:20–21 to "guard the deposit entrusted to you. Avoid the irreverent babble and contradictions of what is falsely called 'knowledge,' for by professing it some have swerved from the faith."

We cannot let anything diminish the glory and greatness of the gospel in our preaching. My hope is that the gospel shines through every part of my sermon and that I can show those in my church how the gospel is the best and only solution to the problem of racism, both on an individual and

---

23. Stott, *Between Two Worlds*, 173.

structural scale. This is where pastoral balance is essential. Neither extreme is healthy, so we must be able to take firm stands, but always with the gospel as our subject and our focus.

Conclusion

In Matt 11:28, Jesus says, "Come to me, all who labor and are heavy laden, and I will give you rest." The gospel answers the problem of injustice. The world cannot because it does not accept that the root of all of the problems we see is our own sin. We must never neglect this or shy away from preaching to the church without exception. But the truth is often dangerous. Those who have been hurt by society, the government, and, unfortunately, the church, deserve to be heard, and those with a voice must speak up for the voiceless. Sin is pervasive and it has caused all sorts of tragedies which harm image bearers of the Creator. We must be able to show how the gospel answers both individual and systemic racism and how an effect of having a gospel-transformed life is to seek justice wherever we see injustice. If our aim as preachers of the gospel is to reach as many people as we can with the truth, we can't shut out people who come to us hurting and suffering.

In the next chapter we will examine how expository preaching fits into a multi-ethnic church. We will dig a little deeper into the idea of dealing with justice issues from the pulpit.

5

How Does Expository Preaching Fit in a Multi-Ethnic Church?

IN CHAPTER 1, WE briefly examined why expository preaching is important for the local church. In this chapter, I will further define what expository preaching is as well as address some of the more common complaints preachers have as reasons for not using this method. In addition, I will show why every preacher needs to connect with as many people as possible in their sermons and how expository preaching is the best way to do that.

What is Expository Preaching?

As previously stated, expository preaching is a term that is widely used, but there are some variations in its usage and definition. The definition I have used so far is that an expository sermon will make the main idea of the passage the main idea of the sermon. A sermon can be one verse or an entire book of the Bible as long as the focus of the biblical passage is the main focus of the sermon. This is the main goal of expository preaching: to expose what the Bible says to the church.

Doing this is more than just a preferred method or style of communication. An expositor chooses to do the hard work of working through difficult books and passages because he has a high view of Scripture. He sees the worth of God's Word as infinitely more valuable than his own ideas or creativity. Helm notes, "Expositional preaching is empowered preaching that rightfully submits the shape and emphasis of the sermon to the shape and emphasis of a biblical text."[1] In other words, the practice of expository preaching is a tangible way to show how the preacher values the Bible because he allows it to drive his sermons. Keller writes, "Expository preaching is the best method for displaying and conveying your conviction that the whole Bible is true. This approach testifies that you believe every part of the Bible to be God's Word, not just particular themes and not just the parts you feel comfortable agreeing with."[2]

A preacher who has a high view of Scripture should be drawn to expository preaching because it values God's Word above all human wisdom. Tony Merida argues, "Preaching, then, is about making God's Word known publicly to a particular audience. More specifically, faithful preaching involves *explaining what God has said in his Word, declaring what God has done in his Son, and applying this message to the hearts of people*. The best approach for accomplishing this agenda is expository preaching."[3] The Word must dictate and direct how we preach and what we preach. Haddon Robinson contends:

> If expository preaching—which is biblical preaching—is the most relevant message we can offer to our hearers, then what do we mean by expository preaching? In the broadest sense, it is preaching that draws its substance from the Scriptures. Actually, true exposition is more of an attitude than a method. It is the honest answer to the questions, "Do I subject my thought to the Scriptures, or do I subject the Scriptures to my thought?" Those are not the same questions as, "Is my sermon theologically orthodox?" (Many orthodox sermons assert a proposition without grounding it in biblical revelation.) Or the question, "Do my sermons contain an assortment of Bible verses?" Or "Is my sermon perceived as coming from the Bible?" It is to ask, "When I approach the Scriptures for a message to preach do I allow the Bible to shape my sermon, or do I let what I have already decided to say determine what I take from the Bible?" Before we stand to speak do we sit and listen to what a passage actually says?[4]

1. Helm, *Expositional Preaching*, 13.
2. Keller, *Preaching*, 32.
3. Merida, *Christ-Centered Expositor*, 9.
4. Robinson, "Relevance of Expository Preaching," 82.

How Does Expository Preaching Fit in a Multi-Ethnic Church?

An expository sermon should always have the biblical text guide the flow of the sermon.

For those who have a high view of Scripture, there is a danger in delivering a sermon that is nothing more than a running commentary. In the next section, I will address a few of those concerns and why some avoid expository preaching, but the truth is that exposition should never be boring. A running commentary is boring to most people as is a bland, dry sermon. An excellent sermon should showcase the gospel (never boring) but it must also connect to the listeners so they can apply the timeless words of Scripture to the problems and difficulties they face. This requires knowing the audience of the biblical text as well as the culture of the modern-day audience. The preacher must be able to build the bridge that spans thousands of years so that the listeners will have something that is relevant and applicable. Anything less does a disservice to both the listener and the Bible because it reduces both to nothing more than an academic talk with no real answers for our problems.

As stated in the previous chapter, the preacher needs to contextualize the passage of Scripture to his audience and culture, but that cannot happen without the preacher first exegeting Scripture. Helm argues:

> All preaching must begin with exegesis. To put it differently: contextualization, theological reflection, and matters of today are held at bay—we should be committed to a process of preparation that *keeps first things first.* By this I mean that a faithful preacher starts the sermon preparation process by paying attention to a biblical text's original audience and a text's purposes for those readers. And he makes this first audience his first concern in three different ways. In one fashion or another, he:
>
> 1. Gives the biblical context (rather than his own context) control over the meaning of the text.
> 2. Listens intently until he knows how the text fits within the overall message of the book.
> 3. Sees the structure and emphasis of the text.
>
> Did you notice how nothing in the above list deals with contextualization? Contextualization is important . . . but good biblical expositors train themselves to hold off that step until later in the process.[5]

---

5. Helm, *Expositional Preaching*, 40.

These two things (scriptural and cultural exegesis) must work in tandem if the preacher is to be faithful to the text and connect with his audience. Kim agrees:

> When we think about tailoring the message for a particular cultural group, some preachers start with people and then try to adapt or modify God's Word to fit the values and perspectives of that cultural context. The danger is that following this model forces the preacher to dart too quickly to application. We are trying to apply the meaning of a passage that we do not understand. In contrast to this view, the starting place in sermon preparation should always be God's Word. We suspend application by first determining the meaning of the text in its context. Once we properly understand what Scripture means, we can then apply it to our varied listeners.[6]

Kim notes that the preacher must begin with hermeneutics and not with the values of the cultural context. He concludes, "If we start with understanding humans today, our preaching and teaching are susceptible to *eisegesis*—reading into the text what is not there, based on our specific cultural lens." According to Kim, the most appropriate thing a preacher can do is begin with God's Word and then apply it to a specific context.[7]

Connecting with the People

As much as expository preaching exalts Jesus Christ, there are risks. To be sure, most of these risks are mitigated by being prepared before stepping into the pulpit and being passionate about the text. The criticisms that preachers sometimes hear do, however, carry some weight. The first complaint that I hear is that expository preaching is often too scholarly or intellectual. I'm certainly not an expert theologian, but I've often said that I could confuse my church rather easily by simply not defining theological terms. Robert Smith contends:

> People come off the streets who have never picked up a Bible. They are often bombarded with these theological words—*justification, sanctification, propitiation, glorification,* and the like. They do not understand these terms. We must not jettison or discard traditional theological terms. They must be rebaptized in the solution of contemporary relevance. The traditional theological dictionary

---

6. Kim, *Preaching with Cultural Intelligence*, 33–34.
7. Kim, *Preaching with Cultural Intelligence*, 33–34.

must remain the same while the contemporary relevant vocabulary and terminology correspond to the precise meaning of the biblical and theological terms.[8]

Any preacher who is well-read can use hefty theological words, but they would only impress those who are either seminary trained or those who have spent a lot of time studying. The overwhelming majority of church members and attendees would be confused, making it difficult to follow the rest of the sermon.

The Sunday morning sermon is not a Ph.D. seminar or a demonstration of the preacher's intellectual capacity. There is certainly truth in the old saying that preachers need to "keep the cookies on the bottom shelf," meaning that the sermon should be accessible to all who are listening, not just the educated or intellectual. Stott aptly notes: "To preach . . . over people's head, is to forget who they are. As Spurgeon once commented, 'Christ said, 'Feed my sheep . . . Feed my lambs.' Some preachers, however, put the food so high that neither lambs nor sheep can reach it. They seem to have the read the text, 'Feed my giraffes.'"[9] A pastor once told me that he thought about a certain person in his church every time he prepared to preach because that person was neither educated nor of high intellect. She loved Jesus, though, and his responsibility to her was to make sure that she learned about Jesus and how to apply the gospel through his preaching. Merida warns against using overly academic language in our preaching: "The overall truth to remember in explaining is to avoid overly academic language. Luther said that when he preached he aimed at the youth in the church, not the highly educated. Refrain from trying to impress people with your personal study. Make the text plain and understandable, so that you teach the text to all of the listeners."[10]

In connecting with the people, the preacher can quickly become consumed with keeping things so simple that he fails to challenge his listeners, thus stunting their growth. I believe that the primary way a church is discipled is through the regular preaching each week, so there must be intellectual challenges for the audience. In other words, the cookies need to be accessible, but they can't stay there. Stott adds:

---

8. Smith Jr., *Doctrine That Dances*, 86.
9. Stott, *Between Two Worlds*, 146–47.
10. Merida, *Christ-Centered Expositor*, 180.

> Although we must not overestimate our congregation's intellectual capacity, we must not underestimate it either. My plea is that we treat them as real people with real questions; that we grapple in our sermons with real issues; and that we build bridges into the real world in which they live and love, work and play, laugh and weep, struggle and suffer, grow old and die. We have to provoke them to think about their life in all its moods, to challenge them to make Jesus Christ the Lord of every area of it, and to demonstrate his contemporary relevance.[11]

The task of every preacher is to know the Bible with enough knowledge to keep people engaged and to know the people enough to speak to the challenges and difficulties they face.

Criticisms of Expository Preaching

Every preaching or teaching style or philosophy will certainly have its detractors. This section will address three points that some give in opposition to expository preaching. They are that it is often too intellectual, that it is too western in its approach, and that it is nothing more than a running commentary. What I will show is that these arguments have validity, but only when the preaching is poorly done. Jerry Vines and Jim Shaddix address this:

> One of the facts of life is that people react against shoddy work. The majority of the criticisms raised against expository preaching are not justified with regard to the approach itself, but they are justified with regard to the approach poorly done. People do not disdain expository preaching; they disdain *poor* expository preaching. Some preachers have fallen prey to certain dangers in expository preaching and have, consequently, abused the approach. These abuses have caused expository preaching to fall into disrepute along the way. Like the careful driver on a well-travelled highway, the pastor will do well to avoid certain potholes along the road to exposition.[12]

Plenty of men go into the pulpit with a great deal of knowledge, correct theology, and solid motives, only to put people to sleep. Expository preaching that is focused on the gospel and teaches the church sound doctrine should never be boring.

---

11. Stott, *Between Two Worlds*, 147.
12. Vines and Shaddix, *Power in the Pulpit*, 37.

How Does Expository Preaching Fit in a Multi-Ethnic Church?

The first common complaint that preachers hear is that expository preaching is often too intellectual. Vines and Shaddix write that simply using exegetical research in the pulpit will frustrate the church. They write, "You cannot afford to take your Bible bullets and toss them at your congregation. You must organize them and then systematically fire them. If you structure your sermon well, you will be far ahead in your attempt to get the biblical message across to a contemporary audience."[13]

In *Black Preaching: The Recovery of a Powerful Art*, Henry Mitchell asserts that one of the main reasons white pastors have such a struggle connecting with black Christians is found in the history of the church. He claims, "It might now be asked why audible response or dialogue disappeared from mainline Protestant patterns of worship. One guess is that the preaching material soared beyond the intellectual reach of the congregation." He notes that worship in white churches and black churches were very similar in the Great Awakenings in the United States, but the intellectual pursuits took white churches beyond where black churches were comfortable going. Mitchell continues:

> This occurred, perhaps, because Protestant seminaries had engaged in a contest of one-upmanship with the graduate division of the liberal arts colleges, creating scholars instead of professionals skilled in reaching people. With such standard conditioning in the theological schools, the preacher might well be expected to be intellectual in concerns rather than interested in the day-to-day issues of ordinary people.[14]

Lenora Tubbs Tisdale, a mainline Protestant like Mitchell, argues that many seminary courses in preaching give far more attention to exegesis of the biblical text than they do to the exegesis of the congregations and contexts. She writes, "The assumption is (erroneously) made that while students need well-defined procedures for exegeting the Scriptures, they can rely on intuition and instinct alone for exegeting congregations."[15] Knowing both the congregation and the community is essential if the preacher wants to avoid being too scholarly.

Jim Scott Orrick, a conservative Baptist, tells a story he heard of an older preacher teaching a younger preacher:

---

13. Vines and Shaddix, *Power in the Pulpit*, 143.
14. Mitchell, *Black Preaching*, 104.
15. Tisdale, *Preaching as Local Theology and Folk Art*, 22–23.

Preaching without Borders

> The older preacher was a southern gentleman, and the younger preacher was what they sometimes call a "boy preacher." Apparently this boy preacher had a pretty sharp mind but did not know how to use it discreetly in the pulpit. The older gentleman said to him, "Boy preacher, you is one of the finest doctrinal preacher I has ever heard. But you are giving the people too much meat. You are going to leave them constipated. You need to throw in a little boonana pudding." For years this story has reminded me to throw in something a little lighter, a little more digestible, a story or a proverb, to help the doctrine "go down."[16]

Putting the "cookies on the bottom shelf" is not dumbing down the text. The skill of being an exceptional expositor is finding the balance between exegesis of the text and exegesis of the people. When these are in the right place, the sermon is challenging and accessible all at the same time.

The second common complaint is that expository preaching is too western in its approach. In other words, expository preaching has a long history of white, European influence. The explanation for the differences between black and white preaching can be found in music. Preaching has a musical quality about it: the tone of voice, rhyme, and cadence all work together to create a harmonious sermon. The difference, however, comes in the very different styles of music that underscore the respective homiletical delivery.

More than a few authors have described the differences in preaching style the same way that jazz is different from classical. Martyn Lloyd-Jones describes preaching as a symphony:

> I maintain that a sermon should have form in the sense that a musical symphony has form. A symphony always has form, it has its parts and its portions. The divisions are clear, and are recognized, and can be described; and yet a symphony is a whole. You can divide it into parts, and yet you always realise that they are parts of a whole, and that the whole is more than the mere summation or aggregate of the parts. One should always think of a sermon as a construction, a work which is in that way comparable to a symphony. In other words a sermon is not a mere meandering through a number of verses; it is not a mere collection or series of excellent and true statements and remarks. All those should be found in the sermon, but they do not constitute a sermon. What makes a sermon a sermon is that it has this particular "form" which differentiates it from everything else.[17]

---

16. Orrick, Payne, and Fullerton, *Encountering God*, 17.
17. Lloyd-Jones, *Preaching and Preachers*, 83.

A listener of a well-crafted and well-delivered sermon can see what Lloyd-Jones means. The sermon is composed of many different points, yet it comes to its crescendo in Christ. Each story and illustration work together like the different instruments in a symphony, all working together to form something organized and harmonious.

White Preaching and Black Preaching

In addressing the differences between a typical white preacher with a typical black preacher, it must be said that those differences do not come strictly from having different preferences. Richards and O'Brien write that the differences are not found in stylistic preferences. Instead, they are ingrained in our culture. They write:

> ... when it comes to communicating the truth, Westerners drift more toward propositions than to artistic expression. Because we are somewhat uncomfortable with the ambiguity of metaphors, we tend to distill propositions out of them. We want to know what they mean, in categorical terms. A philosophical description of God ("omnipresent") is better than an anthropomorphic one ("his eyes roam to and fro throughout the land"). Or so we think. This is why books on Jesus often talk more about the facts of his life than his parables. To us, things like metaphors and parables sometimes seems like unnecessarily frilly packages for a hard truth. We want to get past the packaging to the content; we want to know what it *means*. These assumptions about the value of propositions and our unease with ambiguous language put us at something of a disadvantage when it comes to reading the Bible. The biblical writers didn't make the distinctions we make regarding when metaphorical and potentially ambiguous language is appropriate. We relegate it mainly to informal communication. But the writers of Scripture recorded the profoundest truth in similes, metaphors, parables and other colorful and expressive (and potentially ambiguous) forms of language.[18]

Carl Ellis believes that these differences extend beyond the way that we see the world, and into the way that we see and apply the Bible. He notes:

> If the classical approach to theology has been called "the queen of the sciences," the jazz approach to theology could be called "the queen of the arts." The latter investigates God's dealing with people

---

18. Richards and O'Brien, *Misreading Scripture with Western Eyes*, 84.

in the joys and trial of daily life. This improvisational approach is illustrated in the soul dynamic. The jazz approach is not so much concerned with the status of theological propositions as with the hurts of oppressed people. It is communicated not so much by a literary tradition as by an oral tradition. And it is not so much concerned with facts as it is with life skills: knowing how rather than knowing that.[19]

Over the years, I have heard many white Christians complain that black preaching does not focus as much on theology and doctrine as they would like. While they enjoy the energy and joy that comes from the black preachers they have heard, they often struggle with what they perceive to be the supposed missing element of theological suppositions. In a similar way, many black Christians have said to me that they struggle with white preaching because it is often bland, too intellectual, and it seems to be heavy on truth and light on application. Could these differences that I have observed come from the fact that our cultural differences have brought us to only appreciate one style?

Ellis notes that a difficulty white Americans encounter in many foreign cultures comes from the differences between the classical and jazz mindset. He argues:

> I believe the influence and favor we have with Two-Thirds World nations is God-given. It is also worth noting that most cultures of the Two-Thirds World are jazz-sided like ours. This gives us a distinct advantage in communicating the good news to the world. African-American culture embodies a dynamic system of language. And the African-American experience has enabled our people to more easily establish rapport with Two-Thirds World and oppressed people. Recognizing these facts, mission organizations such as Wycliffe Bible Translators have been asking especially for African-American recruits.[20]

Ellis says that thinking through theology from the perspective of a jazz song can substantially assist white Christians in connecting with different cultures:

> Solid, classical orthodoxy provides limits within which we may improvise, even as musical keys and chord progressions guide jazz musicians. It tells us what God is like and what he is not like. It keeps us from error and excess. However, it does not keep us

---

19. Ellis, Jr., *Free at Last?*, 174.
20. Ellis, Jr., *Free at Last?*, 204–5.

awake, because it does not have the power to blast us out of the "paralysis of analysis."

You may sleep through a symphony, but most people will pay attention to a jazz riff. Jesus calls us to stay awake and be involved in the movements of the times. That is what jazz theology does. It involves us where the "nitty" meets the "gritty." It tells us that God is on the move, that the kingdom is coming. And since the kingdom is coming, it tells us how to get ready. We need to get ready. Our culture is in trouble. Jazz theology can equip us to revive it.[21]

This idea of working through our theology from either a jazz or classical perspective is helpful because it adds color to what we see on the pages of Scripture. Otis Moss observes, "The preacher must approach the text, not with forensic distance, but with artistic passion. The lives of the people, the world of the story, and the pain of the characters must encroach on the consciousness of the preacher and the people. The artistic approach looks at the Bible as a living Word, not a dead scroll."[22]

Black preaching can hardly be described as symphonic. Instead, many scholars of black preaching say that, like much of what is considered black theology, black preaching is much more like jazz than classical music. A white preacher who has attended churches with white pastors and has studied in predominately white schools will most likely be steeped in "classical preaching." That is my story and I see nothing inherently wrong with that. In fact, I am grateful for the training and discipleship that I have received. I appreciate those who have come before me in the Christian faith but I have found that I have only received a partial education. Serving in a church with many who were raised in churches with more "jazz preaching" forced me to consider that I have missed many opportunities to serve others because I was only preaching from my own perspective.

The question that I had to ask was, "Why jazz?" Robert Smith, a teacher of preachers, writes:

> In her book *A Spiritual Biography*, Jana Steed reported that Will Marion Cook, a black classical violinist who became Duke's [Ellington] informal tutor in music theory and composition, advised him to "find the logical way to develop a melody or voice a chord, then go around it and let his 'inner self' break through." Kirk Byron Jones pointed out that Duke Ellington told his band members to play the notes as written but "to keep some dirt in

---

21. Ellis, Jr., *Free at Last?*, 181–82.
22. Moss III, *Blue Note Preaching in a Post-Soul World*, 33–34.

there somewhere." By "dirt" he meant improvisation: spontaneous things they did not plan to do. The Holy Spirit deals in the "dirt area" and provides the preaching with "editing ecstasy." The Holy Spirit robs us of routineness and predictability. The Duke leaves room for some dirt while Lawrence Welk plays every note according to the musical score. When one leaves room for "dirt," the jazz musician no longer plays the notes; the "dirty notes" play the musician. The preachers' responsibility is to take people places they have never been before by being willing to go there themselves. However, this dirt is given license by being first committed to playing the musical score for the basic music. I challenge my students to write every word of the manuscript and then to let the Holy Spirit turn the ink of the manuscript into the blood of spiritual passion.[23]

Smith emphasizes the importance of the preacher to consider different styles when preparing to preach. This is not natural for most people, especially when they have been trained a certain way. He adds, "If there are four beats in a measure, without rehearsing, Europeans will generally clap on the first and third beat. Africans will accent on the offbeat, the second or fourth beat. Most Africans find those beats without rehearsal."[24] For the preacher in a multi-ethnic congregation, this will be difficult. For white preachers, Smith insists that it will be more difficult than for those coming from black churches: ". . . in preaching to white culture, blacks must simply make an adjustment to their beat and feel their liturgical heartbeat. In preaching to black culture, whites must adjust to the rhythm and flow of the congregational atmosphere and allow the congregational current to carry them instead of trying to 'swim upstream against the current.'"[25]

This jazz style preaching will strike some expositors as too extemporaneous for their tastes. In our seminary preaching classes it was drilled into us that we must be prepared, whether that means using a manuscript, outlines, or notes. But does this dichotomy of either being prepared or not being prepared exist at all? Mitchell does not think so. He argues, "Good expositional preaching in any culture will be focused or centered on one main idea and purpose in the passage. The task of the black preacher, again, is simply to make it come alive, as in the outline just given."[26] For Mitchell,

23. Smith, *Doctrine That Dances*, 153.
24. Smith, *Doctrine That Dances*, 149.
25. Smith, *Doctrine That Dances*, 149.
26. Mitchell, *Black Preaching*, 117.

How Does Expository Preaching Fit in a Multi-Ethnic Church?

the sermon involves the listeners as much as the preacher: "If it is a letter from Paul to the difficult church at Corinth, then the preacher will get into Paul's head and worry about what's going on in Corinth. Then, thinking out loud, the preacher will write the letter-sermon." The entire congregation will join with the preacher.[27] This is uncomfortable for many "classical" preachers, but we must be willing to sacrifice our comfort so that we reach more people with the truth of the gospel.

For preachers who are correctly focused on preaching doctrinally rich sermons, making these adjustments will often be difficult. Any time we step out of our comfort zone we experience challenges. These "growing pains" mean that we are maturing as preachers and that we are beginning to understand what preaching without borders really means. Smith argues that this is exactly what Jesus did. He argues:

> Doctrinal preaching, more than any other kind of preaching, is likely to be heavy in complex, technical, and theological language. Jesus used parables to transmit His doctrine and to carry home His teachings. The parables are saturated with doctrine, but they are theology in pictures. A major element and ingredient in the Lord's doctrinal preaching and teaching ministry was His use of images. When Jesus used parables as a teaching device, He was essentially using secular stories, not Sunday school stories, to illustrate and unfold sacred secrets of the kingdom of God. These parables were designed to do more than inform the mind; they were intended to provide the hearers with a picture to hang on the walls in the gallery of their minds. Jesus told parables to supply both visual and aural special effects; He wanted people to see and hear God, themselves, and others.[28]

Jazz preaching is painting pictures with our words. It is taking what the Bible says and explaining it in a way that people can visualize what it must have been like for Jesus in the Garden of Gethsemane or Paul at the Areopagus. The listeners need to have their minds challenged but they also need to feel a connection.

The common criticism of expository preaching is that it is so focused on the mind that emotions or imagination are left behind. Smith warns against this:

---

27. Mitchell, *Black Preaching*, 118.
28. Smith, *Doctrine That Dances*, 67–68.

> As doctrinal preachers, we need to be liberated from the sterile and predictable language used in our preaching. This language is more like dusting plastic flowers than cultivating roses. The doctrinal preacher needs to use language that is similar to the language of the Bible—language that has elasticity and portability for use in our contemporary times.[29]

Tisdale calls this "engaging in a dance of the imagination." For her, the preacher joins hands with other partners—the Bible, congregational context, doctrine. The preacher "dances" with these things until a "local theology emerges." Rather than being rigid and uniform (as we see in classical music), "the preacher as dancer is given freedom to attend to the various partners, and to discern in each new setting in time and place where to begin the dance toward a sermon, and how to proceed." This is all done to ensure that the sermon brings scriptural truths into the contexts of the local congregation.[30]

The third common complaint is that expository preaching is nothing more than a running commentary. In other words, the sermon is boring. Most preachers enjoy reading commentaries and books that discuss what the Bible says, and most preachers want to give as much information as possible about the text to the congregation. Some preachers, however, fall back to regurgitating the deep truths of Scripture with very little material with which to engage anyone but the intellectual. Vines and Shaddix give the following advice:

> We have a message that is eminently worthy of being heard and received. We must so present that message that it will be interesting and appealing to those who hear us. Some would say our job is not to make the gospel appealing but to make it available. But we are not faced with such an alternative. Rather, we are called to greater effectiveness in delivery so that we can make the gospel appealing as we make it available. Work hard to make the Bible come alive in your stylistic expression. You will discover that your listeners will become much more interested in your sermons.[31]

The gospel is the most exciting thing any Christian preacher can talk about so each sermon should be full of passion and joy. To be fair, every preacher has a unique style and personality, so I am not saying that we all need to

---

29. Smith, *Doctrine That Dances*, 73.
30. Tisdale, *Preaching as Local Theology and Folk Art*, 92.
31. Vines and Shaddix, *Power in the Pulpit*, 260.

have the theatrics of Billy Sunday or T.D. Jakes. A wild performance will often take away from the message being preached, but there must be energy in the delivery of the sermon. If we believe that the Bible is the inerrant Word of God and that it has the power to change our lives, we must preach as if the life of our church depends on it. Smith notes:

> Since God created humans, should not that realm of the human construct be allowed to participate in the sending and receiving of the Word of God? John Wesley was once asked why so many people came to hear him preach. His response was, "When you set yourself on fire, people love to come and see you burn." Preaching must be doxological and not boring.[32]

A running commentary may get the doctrinal and exegetical aspect of the text correct but preaching demands that the preacher set himself "on fire" so that those listening can see the burning of the gospel.

Answering the Common Complaints

Not every complaint against using expository preaching in a multi-ethnic church can be listed here, but the above examples are perhaps the most common preachers will hear. This section will address those criticisms with practical ways that the preacher can use to make his sermon and delivery more engaging. No matter how substantial our points may be, if we are not holding the attention of the congregation, our message will fall flat for most people. Stephen McQuoid gives the preacher the following advice:

> Today's preacher needs to hold the concentration of his audience. This may involve using a variety of styles in his preaching, the use of good illustrations and visual aids, and being creative in his presentation. He also needs to preach in such a way as to make his audience think about the message and evaluate it. There is no point in preaching if it goes in one ear of his listeners and then immediately out the other. His preaching must provoke thought and a response. He must also preach such spiritually enriching sermons that they actively combat the permissive attitudes which his listeners have imbibed in this television centered culture.[33]

---

32. Smith, *Doctrine That Dances*, 104.
33. McQuoid, *Beginner's Guide to Expository Preaching*, 20–21.

Preaching without Borders

I believe that every preacher who desires to see people grow in their faith will agree with McQuoid's statement but many will question what to do about it. The following are some statements that preachers may find helpful in crafting sermons that connect with listeners across all ethnic barriers.

The first thing a preacher can do is to be a story-teller. With so much focus on the explanation of the Scripture, we can easily forget that the entire Bible is the story of God's plan to glorify himself. The preacher should think of himself as an artist who is painting a verbal picture of what he sees in the Bible. What was Paul doing and what did he feel as he wrote to the Corinthian believers? How did they feel as they read the letters? What terror and encouragement did the Christians feel as they read John's Revelation? When we explain what the Bible says with vivid imagery and imagination, we will hold the attention of our listeners. Since the entire Bible is God's story, we ought to be superb story-tellers. Roger Van Harn contends:

> It [God's story] comes to us in the Bible, which spans many centuries and can be traced through vast cultural changes. From the journeys of Abraham to Israel's oppression in Egypt to the exodus, the wilderness, and the promised land, God's Story has already happened in and through cultural changes—and it has only just begun. The days of the judges, kings, prophets, exile in Babylon, and restoration weave the Story through changing scenes that seem to have little in common. The New Testament begins in the days of Caesar Augustus, whose collection of taxes set the stage for the birth of Jesus in Bethlehem, and it ends with the apostle John in exile on the Isle of Patmos, singing new songs about the victory of the Lamb who was slain. The Story is told in and through many cultural changes but is never limited or reduced to anyone. The way we receive God's Story in the Bible gives a clue as to how it is possible for us to see our own culture in its light.[34]

This protects us from the dangers of reading into the text things that are not there. Van Harn adds, "Nothing helps us see our own culture better than seeing ourselves through the eyes of people from different cultures. As we bring our cultures to God's Story together, we will see more clearly, enabled to avoid confusing our culture with God's Story."

Being a story-teller helps us to better explain the biblical text while not allowing the current culture to dominate our interpretations, but it also helps us to connect with the culture as well. Tisdale proclaims that telling stories makes the Bible accessible to the common person. She writes,

---

34. Van Harn, *Preacher, Can You Hear Us Listening?*, 84.

"Rather than aiming for the grandiose, the miraculous, and the extraordinary in illustrative materials, such preaching strives to enflesh the gospel in real-life stories about real-life people in real-life situations with which a local congregation can identify."[35]

Another aspect of story-telling is the testimony of the preacher. Just as most cultures appreciate an engaging message with a story laced throughout, most cultures appreciate knowing the story of the man behind the sermon. The congregation needs to know how the preacher came to know Christ and how the gospel has changed him forever. Smith argues that personal testimony is a way to make doctrinal preaching come alive. He notes:

> People do not just want to know that God brought Daniel out of the lion's den. They want to know if the preacher has ever been in the lion's den and experienced God's delivering power. Three times Paul's testimony about his conversion experience is given in the book of Acts. The tribulation saints overcame persecution by the blood of the Lamb and by their testimony (Rev 12:11). The preacher's testimony must be a servant of the text and never seek to master or take over the text. The testimony will have power when it reinforces the message of the text; it will lose power when it gives a message that is antithetical to the text. God has promised to bless His Word about Himself and not necessarily our words about Him. But the preacher's testimony that is consistent with the interpretation and message of the text will provide encouragement and edification for the congregation.[36]

To give some balance to the above quotation, Smith warns about committing "ecclesiastical nudity" from the pulpit by being overly transparent with the congregation. He concludes, "People do not necessarily need to 'see through you' to know that God has 'seen you through.'"[37] As with so much of the Christian life, there is a balance that must be found between sharing so much that people are turned off to our preaching and being too "pure" that people are surprised when we sin.

---

35. Tisdale, *Preaching as Local Theology and Folk Art*, 130.
36. Smith, *Doctrine That Dances*, 117–18.
37. Smith, *Doctrine That Dances*, 117–18.

Preaching without Borders

Speaking the Language of the People

Speaking the language of the community is a practical way to combat the possible pitfalls of expository preaching. This may mean learning a new language. Think of the goodwill for the gospel that could be accomplished if a church, stirred by the leadership, devotes itself to learn a new language so that it can serve the community better. The ministry of the pulpit is no different. When someone hears their pastor making an attempt to communicate better with the congregation and community, the people will pay attention to his preaching and leadership. But speaking the language of a community goes deeper than learning vocabulary and syntax. It involves the tenor (what you say) and tone (how you say it).

In previous chapters I have addressed the need to know one's audience. One would be hard-pressed to find a book on either preaching or public speaking that does not include at least some cursory advice about knowing something about who is listening. Here I want to go a bit deeper in terms of not just knowing *who* is listening, but also knowing *how* they listen. Public speaking resources will address this, but Christian preachers ought to take this a step further because we are not trying to sell something. We are not motivational speakers. We have the life-changing message of the gospel and our attitude should always be that of Charles Spurgeon, when he delivered an oft-quoted statement: "If sinners will be damned, at least let them leap to hell over our bodies! And if they will perish, let them perish with our arms about their knees, imploring them to stay, and not madly to destroy themselves! If hell must be filled, at least let it be filled in the teeth of our exertions, and let not one go there unwarned and unprayed for!"[38] If we believe this, we will be ready and willing to make changes in our preaching to ensure that the gospel is clearly heard.

Since we have a message that is greater than every other message, it is essential for us to be clear. For that to happen, we have to speak in a way that people will understand what we say and what we mean. Preaching professor Fred Craddock wrote:

> Giving disciplined time and attention to the interpretation of one's listeners is critical for preaching. It in no way diminishes the importance of careful exegesis of texts, but then neither does any amount of work in a text make a sermon apart from this understanding. No book of theology, even if it is addressed to the modern mind; no

---

38. Spurgeon, "Wailing of Risca," 22–40.

How Does Expository Preaching Fit in a Multi-Ethnic Church?

biblical commentary, even if it moves the text toward the pulpit; no volume of sermons, packaged and ready for delivery, has the Word winged for the hearts and minds of a particular group of listeners. Only the minister there can properly do that.[39]

Craddock advocates that a preacher spend time studying the congregation so that his sermon will resonate with as many people as possible. Tisdale agrees and says that pastors have been shortchanged in seminaries, where the focus is on exegesis of the text while exegesis of the congregation is neglected. She remarks that seminaries teach pastors to begin with the text and then move on to the themes of the text. Only after this, she says, pastors are trained to work on application and how the sermon will connect with the congregation. Tisdale takes Craddock's statement many steps further by advocating for the preacher to begin sermon preparation not with the biblical text but rather with the audience in mind.[40] But the expositor cannot begin with the audience because he has been charged to "preach the Word." We must begin with what the Bible says. When a preacher follows the well-intentioned, but misguided, advice of professors like Tisdale, he is placing more emphasis on people than on God's Word.

Even though we do not give the exegesis of the community or congregation first importance, we still value the people when we prepare and preach a sermon. Vines and Shaddix write that there is "electricity" that flows between the preacher and the people and that that electricity is a mark of many of the great expositors. They write, "This spark between preacher and people must be present if preaching is to accomplish its intended end."[41] This "electricity" can often be found in black churches, where the congregation "talks back" to the preacher. In referencing Henry Mitchell's work, Stott says that black Americans "have been free in their worship to express authentically black selfhood. Black religion is 'soul religion,' unafraid of emotion and ecstasy."[42] According to Mitchell, this call and response between preacher and congregation has gone on for centuries in Africa and in black churches in the United States from their infancy.[43]

The call and response heard in many black churches is similar to what can be heard from Baptist and Pentecostal preachers in the American

---

39. Craddock, *Preaching*, 92.
40. Tisdale, *Preaching as Local Theology and Folk Art*, 95.
41. Vines and Shaddix, *Power in the Pulpit*, 311.
42. Stott, *Between Two Worlds*, 60.
43. Mitchell, *Recovery of Preaching*, 116.

South. There is an awareness of the congregation to the preacher and of the preacher to the congregation, which seems out of place for many who are unfamiliar with an audience being "noisy" during a presentation. The shouting from both preacher and pew is the outflowing of heartfelt worship. Vines and Shaddix write, "Their worship services are unashamedly emotional and expressive. True audience participation occurs. The worshipers actually talk back to the preacher. He knows how to pace himself accordingly. He leads in two-way communication." This communication that goes back and forth gives the preacher inspiration and stimulation. "He soars to the heights as he delivers the sermon."[44]

Learning to speak the language of the people takes great attention and hard work, but this is necessary if we aim to reach more people for the gospel. Seminary president Timothy Tennent claims one way we can do this is by listening to voices outside of the western church. He gives the following example: "Western preaching and theologizing can sometimes drift into a static state whereby we teach truths without engaging in the missional context of the church. This is not true of African preaching."[45] He then quotes Dutch missiologist Johannes Verkuyl: "African theology does all the things which theology in general does, but in African theology all these other functions are embraced in a missionary or communicative function. It is not primarily an inter-ecclesiastical exercise, but a discipline driven by . . . active evangelization."[46] Tisdale suggests that preachers are often "unaware and unprepared" because they have been trained in theology but not in cross-cultural missions. She contends:

> *Unaware* because it is easy to assume that people who speak the same language and live in the same country and belong to the same denomination as we do are, to a large extent, "like" us. And *unprepared* because, on the whole, seminary courses and texts in homiletics have not adequately acknowledged the cross-cultural dimensions of the preaching task, and have frequently done a far better job of training future pastors to exegete Scripture than of teaching them to "exegete" and probe the depths of hidden meaning within local congregations and their subcultures.[47]

---

44. Vines and Shaddix, *Power in the Pulpit*, 311.
45. Tennent, "Evangelical Preaching in the Global Context," 206.
46. Verkuyl, *Contemporary Missiology*, 277.
47. Tisdale, *Preaching as Local Theology and Folk Art*, 30.

How Does Expository Preaching Fit in a Multi-Ethnic Church?

Perhaps the long-term solution to this would be for seminary students to take more classes specifically aimed at ministry to people outside of their own culture. Another suggestion would be for pastors to view themselves more as a missionary; as someone who is a sojourner in Babylon rather than a citizen of wherever they may live.

Recognizing one's own deficiencies requires thick skin and an ability to see their work honestly. One of the more difficult things that I experienced as a first-time preaching pastor in a multi-ethnic church was removing colloquialisms and idioms from my preaching. We do not think much about these things because we use them so much. Someone in Boston might say that the Red Sox game was "wicked awesome," thoroughly confusing a Southerner. Someone from Alabama might describe something as "cattywampus," meaning that something was messed up or sideways. Idioms are even more difficult to decipher. An adult who has lived their entire life in the United States would have no difficulty understanding what "beating around the bush" or "don't upset the apple cart" means, but to someone who is not a native English speaker, these will make no sense at all.

In casual conversation, these colloquialisms and idioms are appealing. It's part of the reason we travel to other countries; we want to experience authentic communication. For Americans, the folksiness of certain phrases is often appealing, but in a sermon where different nations, regions, ethnicities, or class are present, these statements become something else altogether: they confuse the audience and limit the impact of the sermon. Even people in the same community will have different ways of speaking. This is perhaps the most challenging aspect of preaching to an audience of "differents." Pastor and professor Zack Eswine gives the following example of communication breakdown:

> Imagine a pastor from Ghana visiting a pastor in Ukraine at the beginning of winter. The pastor from Ghana begins to bundle up with warm clothes. The Ukranian pastor smiles. He tries to convey to his Ghanaian friend that, as cold as it may presently seem, time will bring vastly colder conditions. "The weather will descend to 0 degrees," he says. But the pastor from Ghana has no concept of what this precision means. "It will get very, very cold," the Ukrainian says with ordinary language. But this approach falls short of the purpose as well. The purpose is to help his friend get a sense of what it will be like when things get colder, so he says, "In a few weeks, the cold, the wind, and the snow will join forces and attack

you. They will reach through your clothing and taunt your skin so that you shiver beyond control in order to get warm."[48]

The above story shows the frustration that often happens in cross-cultural communication.

When I first began my ministry at a small, multi-ethnic church in Florida, I taught through the book of James. In the introduction to my sermon from Jas 1:26–27, I gave three Spanish idioms and their translations. The first was *tiene mas lana que un borrego*, which is translated as "he has more wool than a lamb," meaning that a person has money to waste. The second was *como el burro que toco la flauta*, which is "as the donkey plays the flute," somehow meaning that something happened by pure luck. Finally, I gave an idiom that many in the church said described themselves: *no tener pelos en la lengua*, which in English is someone who "does not have hairs on their tongue." In other words, the person always says what they are thinking.[49] Pastoring a church with many Spanish speakers was a learning experience to say the least. In chapter 8, I will share some practical advice to preachers about how to avoid these confusing statements from the pulpit and how to improve in cultural awareness.

Preaching About Difficult Subjects

Expository preaching, when done well, fits into a multi-ethnic church because it forces the preacher to address difficult subjects. Because of the expositor's commitment to preaching through books of the Bible, difficult topics cannot be skipped or avoided. Pastor Ryan Huguley argues, "As preachers, we are often averse to preaching difficult, confusing, controversial, or awkward topics. If you choose to be an expository preacher, and especially if you preach verse by verse through entire books of the Bible, you won't have the luxury of skipping topics. If it's in the text, you'll have to deal with it."[50] H.B. Charles holds that consecutive exposition of Scripture not only forces us to preach topics that are difficult, but it also gives us protection against the accusation that we are preaching at people. He adds, "If a difficult word is preached, your defense is that you were only working

---

48. Eswine, *Preaching to a Post-Everything World*, 107.
49. Ryan Roach, "Acceptable Religion."
50. Huguley, *8 Hours or Less*, 26.

with the text that was in front of you. It would be irresponsible to skip over something you would rather not say."[51]

A church where I pastored needed some extra income so we decided to rent out our building on Sunday afternoons to a church plant. One church that used our facility was pastored by a man with no formal training or experience. His only ministerial experience came from occasionally speaking at revivals or retreats. One day, he came to me for some preaching advice, saying that he needed some help with his preparation and planning, so I agreed to help him. He asked for my sermon schedule and some manuscripts to help him be more organized and, a few weeks later, he told me that he had used my preaching schedule as a guide and that he had begun preaching through the book of James. I was excited that he was seeing the fruit of expository preaching until he told me that he skipped over Jas 1:26–27 because he had a few known gossips in his church and he did not want to make them upset. I pleaded with him to let the Bible speak for itself but this pastor decided to stop meeting with me at that point. He misunderstood the purpose and importance of letting the Bible speak for itself. Orrick et al. rhetorically ask, "How many topical preachers have preached Genesis 36, the genealogy of Esau? Or, how many have preached Judges 19, the 'Levite and his concubine?' But are those texts also the Word of God? Are those texts profitable?" They write that preaching through books of the Bible will stretch the preacher and his congregation, as both will be forced to deal with issues that are not easy or comfortable.[52]

Some of these difficult issues include race, ethnicity, and justice. Theologically conservative white pastors have largely failed at addressing these issues. Our brothers and sisters of color have experienced great harm done in the name of Jesus. Soong-Chan Rah insists, "During the time when African-Americans were pursuing justice and civil rights, many evangelical white congregations remained on the sidelines. By failing to stand for justice and opting to ignore injustice in society for the sake of focusing on the salvation of individual souls, many of the white churches lost credibility in the black community."[53] The tension that many pastors face when addressing issues of systemic or structural racism are not new. The philosophical ground that we walk today was laid many years ago. Rah recognizes this

---

51. Charles Jr., *Preaching*, 61.
52. Orrick et al., *Encountering God*, 70–71.
53. Rah, *Many Colors*, 56.

stained history: "Because of the failure of many (not all) in the white church to stand against injustice, the rift between black and white grew." Rah notes that these historical failures provide obstacles for ministry even today and that cultural intelligence requires knowing our sordid past.[54]

Expository preaching will force the preacher to confront these issues. For example, if we are preaching through the Proverbs, we will have to address Prov 31:8–9: "Open your mouth for the mute, for the rights of all who are destitute. Open your mouth, judge righteously, defend the rights of the poor and needy." Another verse that would certainly require contextualization and possibly controversial application is Prov 14:31: "Whoever oppresses a poor man insults his Maker, but he who is generous to the needy honors him."

There are many passages in Scripture that speak to issues that plague us today; there is nothing new under the sun. But even seeing these in Scripture, there are accusations that are sometimes charged against preachers who address issues of justice and racism from the pulpit. The common advice that many of us have heard is to "just preach the gospel." While I fully agree that the gospel must be at the center of everything we do, we cannot forget that applying the gospel to problems that we see in Scripture and in the world is part of the job of the expositor. In other words, preaching the gospel demands that the preacher apply the gospel. Carl Ellis recounts that Martin Luther King, Jr. was accused of not preaching the gospel. He notes:

> Dr. King was also criticized for not preaching the gospel and not getting people saved. But we can't always preach the gospel at sixty-five miles an hour. When road and weather conditions are bad, we have to slow down to a safe or understandable speed. In the case of the Civil Rights Movement the goal was to eliminate segregation (to apply the gospel at five miles per hour). How did the Civil Rights Movement relate to the gospel? Segregation points to racism; racism points to human depravity; depravity points to human rebellion against God; rebellion brings God's judgment and wrath; judgment points to our need for salvation; and our need for salvation points to Jesus Christ, our only hope for it. Martin Luther King Jr. applied the Word of God to the evils manifested in society without letting us forget that Jesus was the ultimate fulfillment of the Civil Rights Movement.[55]

54. Rah, *Many Colors*, 56.
55. Ellis, Jr., *Free at Last?*, 87.

Ellis argues that King was preaching the gospel, just not in the exact way that many in conservative evangelical circles prefer. The modern-day expositor has plenty of ills in society to address through the preaching of God's word. Again, it's not adding to the gospel; it is correctly applying it.

Conclusion

In the first few years of ministry I was almost entirely focused on teaching theology and making sure that people thought correctly about the Bible. This is certainly one of the primary aspects of pastoral ministry, but it is not the only one. The pastors I admired most were theologically astute; they had a command of Scripture and doctrine, but that was the only aspect of their ministry that I saw. So, like so many young upstarts, I became so dogmatic in my theological preaching that I failed to be a gentle shepherd. I taught like my heroes but I failed to lovingly pastor the people.

In the years since I have seen that my preaching ministry needs to be a combination of head, heart, and hands. I must be sure to preach to the intellect and to the emotions, as well as to motivate people to go and do something about what they just learned and felt. It is Romans and James joining to celebrate the gospel. Jeffrey Arthurs, preaching professor at Gordon Conwell Theological Seminary, observes in his book *Preaching as Reminding*, that one can preach to the mind with solid exegesis, but miss the heart. His entire work focuses on the job of the preacher to stir the memory of those listening so that the gospel shines in their hearts and minds. He notes, "Reminding may seem to be primarily a cognitive function of preaching, but it actually has just as much to do with emotion as cognition." The preacher rouses the sleeping knowledge of the people with the fire that comes through the preached Word of God.[56] Arthurs concludes that the preacher must stir the imagination of the listener through vivid language, which "captures attention and compels assent by causing the mind to process information in ways that correspond to actual sensory experience."[57]

I have also experienced another change in my preaching. I have learned (often through many mistakes) that if I hope to connect with people across all borders (ethnic, man-made, or otherwise), I must do the hard work of faithfully preaching through God's Word and do it without all the trappings

---

56. Arthurs, *Preaching as Reminding*, 57.
57. Arthurs, *Preaching as Reminding*, 66–67.

that were discussed in this chapter. In the next chapter, we will explore what expository preaching can do in a multi-ethnic congregation.

6

Possibilities of Preaching to a Multi-Ethnic Church

PREACHING TO A CHURCH that is diverse, as we have seen, is certainly not easy. There are many pitfalls that a preacher can fall into if he does not take great care of his soul. He can also get into trouble if he does not craft his sermons with a focus on the gospel and proclaiming the glory of God. The aim of this chapter is to demonstrate the positive effects of preaching to a multi-ethnic church.

Three Audiences

Before turning our attention to the positive effects of preaching to a multi-ethnic church, we need to consider the three audiences to whom we preach. The reason for this is that while preachers often consider all three audiences when preparing and delivering a sermon, the tendency for many preachers is to fall back on what is comfortable to them. In the following paragraphs, we will see who the three audiences of our worship are (preaching is included) and why we must master each of them.

In his book *Rhythms of Grace*, pastor Mike Cosper describes our worship as having three audiences. These three audiences are: "God, who is both the object of our praise and a witness to us as we praise him; there is the church, which both participates in and witnesses the lives and gatherings of the people; and there is the world, watching from the darkness."[1] There are dangers in confusing or overemphasizing these audiences. For our worship to accomplish its purpose, we need to focus on who we are singing about at the same time we seek to build up the church and be gospel witnesses to those who are not believers.

Cosper's work focuses on the whole of worship with an emphasis on singing and the importance of liturgy. Here, in this book, the focus is on preaching though the same advice applies. What follows in this chapter is an argument that our preaching must connect with the three audiences: God, the church, and the world. Tim Keller, who has served as an example to many preachers, writes:

> In the end, preaching has two basic objects in view: the Word and the human listener. It is not enough to just harvest the wheat; it must be prepared in some edible form or it can't nourish and delight. Sound preaching arises out of two loves—love of the Word of God and love of people—and from them both a desire to show people God's glorious grace. And so, while only God can open hearts, the communicator must give great time and thought both to presenting the truth accurately and to bringing it home to the hearts and lives of the hearers.[2]

While he does not frame his argument using the same terminology of Cosper, Keller's understanding of preaching fits into the tripartite idea of worship posited by Cosper. The preacher must seek to glorify God, give exhortation and exposition to the church, and present the gospel clearly for the world to hear.

The first audience of our preaching is God. Paul's charge to Timothy to "preach the word; be ready in season and out of season," is not contingent on having a large congregation or even one at all. In fact, 2 Tim 4:3–4 says, "For the time is coming when people will not endure sound teaching, but having itching ears they will accumulate for themselves teachers to suit their own passions, and will turn away from listening to the truth and wander off into myths." We are to preach the word in season and out, even if people have tuned us out or we have lost our congregation. God's Word "is living and active, sharper than any two-edged sword, piercing to the division of soul and of spirit, of joints and of marrow, and discerning

---

1. Cosper, *Rhythms of Grace*, 83.
2. Keller, *Preaching*, 14.

the thoughts and intentions of the heart (Hebrews 4:12)." It does not matter how many are in attendance. What matters most is whether we are being faithful to the Word of God and teaching in alignment with Scripture. God is our first audience and we must seek to honor him.

The second audience is the local church. The seeker-driven movement, where churches focus their ministry on outreach and attracting a crowd, often downplays the church as the second audience and sometimes fails to even consider God as the first. Steven Furtick, pastor of Elevation Church in Charlotte, NC, has been known for his focus on growing his church numerically and as his church attendance was growing rapidly, he addressed the growing number of concerned Christians who questioned his methods. In one sermon, he said, "If you know Jesus, I'm sorry to break it to you, this church [Elevation] is not for you. *'Yeah, but last week, I gave my life to Christ at Elevation.'* Last week was the last week that Elevation Church existed for you."[3] Furtick and so many others have made evangelism during Sunday morning worship a priority over equipping the saints.

What Furtick and others do well, however, is that they have a great understanding of what matters to people. They can speak the language of the people in the church and the community so that their message is clear and the people respond. H.B. Charles, writing about crafting an effective introduction, notes that the preacher must know his congregation if he is to have any effect:

> You should know whom you are preaching to, as well as what you are preaching about. Then craft your introduction for your listeners. Seek to grab the attention of the congregation from the beginning. I admit this is easier if you preach to the same congregation each week. If you are a consistent preacher, your congregation will give you the benefit of the doubt and wait to see where the sermon is going. But don't take them for granted. Keep them on their toes by engaging them in the introduction. If you are preaching in an unfamiliar setting, it is all the more important to make a connection as quickly as possible. Appeal to commonalities, and avoid unnecessary offense.[4]

Charles is a master at connecting across racial and ethnic divides. His preaching is passionate while remaining faithful in his exposition. His skill comes from knowing Scripture and his church, as well as the community.

---

3. "Steven Furtick—Elevation 'Church' Is Not For Believers."
4. Charles, *Preaching*, 81–82.

Preaching without Borders

The third audience is the world. This will sometimes be elevated above the audience of the church to the detriment of the believers in the congregation. While the desire to reach the lost is admirable, the order of these audiences is not accidental. My primary duty as a preacher of the Word is to glorify God through the building up of the saints. Evangelism is an important element in the preaching of Scripture, but it should never rise above the first two.

With that said, it may now seem strange that I encourage preachers to preach in view of the world. We must keep those who are not Christians in our minds as we prepare and preach, but they must never be our main audience during worship on the Lord's Day. An effective expositional sermon will address the gospel as the answer to the main problem that everyone in the room faces, whether they follow Christ or not. Our sin has separated every one of us from God, but Jesus Christ, through his perfect life and sacrificial death, has lived and died for us so we could be made right with God and not suffer his wrath. Christians need to be reminded of this and those outside of the faith need to hear this message of freedom. In addressing what exceptional preaching is, Keller states:

> It is also proclaiming to *"both Jews and Greeks"* (1 Corinthians 1:24)—preaching compellingly, engaging the culture, and touching hearts. This means not merely informing the mind but also capturing the hearer's interest and imagination and persuading her toward repentance and action. A good sermon is not like a club that that beats upon the will but like a sword that cuts to the heart (Acts 2:37). At its best it pierces to our very foundations, analyzing and revealing us to ourselves (Hebrews 4:12). It must build on Bible exposition, for people have not understood a text unless they see how it bears on their lives. Helping people see this is the task of *application*, and it is much more complicated than is usually recognized. As we have said, preaching to the heart and to the culture are linked, because cultural narratives profoundly affect each individual's sense of identity, conscience, and understanding of reality. Cultural engagement in preaching must never be for the sake of appearing "relevant" but rather must be for the purpose of laying bare the listener's life foundations.[5]

Kim contends that preachers in a church with a variety of cultures must ask a few questions of themselves if they want to be successful in preaching without borders. He adds:

5. Keller, *Preaching*, 21.

Possibilities of Preaching to a Multi-Ethnic Church

> As preachers, we want to pursue and reflect on life and Scripture from the Others' viewpoint. For example, have you ever asked yourself these questions about your listeners during sermon preparation? (1) How would listeners from Life Situation X or from Cultural Background Y read and interpret this Scripture passage? (2) What excites them, and what do they fear? (3) Which illustrations are most relevant and helpful for these listeners? (4) What does life application look like in their specific context? (5) How can we embrace and even celebrate those who are different from us in our preaching ministry and in "doing life" together?[6]

Considering others, especially those outside of our own cultural, ethnic, socioeconomic group, is hard work. It takes a great deal of cultural intelligence, and that requires energy and effort as well as the opportunities to make mistakes and learn from them.

It is easier for the preacher to rest on what he knows because it is safer, at least in the sense that he will likely not offend the cultural norms of the listeners. In my experience with fellow preachers, I have found that many of us want to grow our church and have more people hear the gospel, but we seem to be preaching only to Christians each week. Being effective means knowing the audience. Max Atkinson, an educator and expert in public speaking, claims:

> The problem of public speaking, in all its various manifestations, lies in a profound and widespread misunderstanding of how spoken communication works. At the heart of this is a failure to appreciate that there are important differences between speaking to an audience and other much more familiar forms of communication, notably everyday conversation and the language of the written word. Somewhere along the line, speakers seem to have stopped thinking about the needs and preferences of their audiences.[7]

When we fail to recognize that the church is made up of believers but, at the same time, non-Christians will attend, our preaching will be skewed to one extreme or another, causing either a "holy huddle" or an evangelistic crusade, neither of which is healthy or biblical.

Preaching that considers the three audiences (God, the church, the world) demands that the preacher know who God is (theology) and who the church is (pastoral care). There are many resources that focus on how

---

6. Kim, *Preaching with Cultural Intelligence*, xiii.
7. Atkinson, *Lend Me Your Ears*, 14.

these work in tandem. The third audience is a focus of missiology. Knowing the culture in which one ministers is essential if the missionary or church planter is to find success. What this book has attempted to do so far is show that the preacher must work to master all three of these audiences. This matters to the preacher because he likely was not raised in a multi-ethnic congregation and because, frankly, having a wider worldview in terms of culture and ethnicity does not come naturally to most people.

What Can Happen When Expository Preaching is Unleashed in a Multi-Ethnic Context

Salt and Light in a Dark and Dying World

Faithful exposition of Scripture in a multi-ethnic church will allow us to be, to use the words of Christ, salt and light to the world. In the Sermon on the Mount, he says in Matt 5:13–16 (ESV):

> You are the salt of the earth, but if salt has lost its taste, how shall its saltiness be restored? It is no longer good for anything except to be thrown out and trampled under people's feet. You are the light of the world. A city set on a hill cannot be hidden. Nor do people light a lamp and put it under a basket, but on a stand, and it gives light to all in the house. In the same way, let your light shine before others, so that they may see your good works and give glory to your Father who is in heaven.

A reading of the text leading up to this passage could be used to justify living like the Amish, but not in these four verses. New Testament scholar Craig Blomberg observes that since salt was used as a preservative, Jesus is telling his followers to "arrest corruption and prevent moral decay in their world." For something to lose its saltiness is not to lose flavor. Instead, it was to become defiled.[8] When Jesus speaks about being "the light of the world," he is saying that since he is the Light of the world, his followers should reflect that. Blomberg continues, "Like lights from a city illuminating the dark countryside or a lamp inside a house providing light for all within it, Christians must let their good works shine before the rest of the world so that others may praise God. The good works are most naturally seen as the 'fruits in keeping with repentance' of [Matthew] 3:8."[9] Jesus is saying

---

8. Blomberg, *Matthew*, 102.
9. Blomberg, *Matthew*, 103.

that Christians are to be actively involved in our world, not just to make it a better place for the sake of making it better, but to make it better by encouraging others to follow God's standards. This is an outward response of being changed by the gospel.

The tangible effect of obedience to the words of Christ in Matthew 5 and in the Great Commission in Matthew 28 combined with the emphasis on the importance of the local church throughout the New Testament is that Christians see the value in community and especially one that is diverse in ethnicity and background. When I pastored a diverse church in Orlando, FL, about a third of our church was Latino. Even though Latinos did not comprise the majority of our church, they were the dominate culture. Our potlucks were mostly Latin food, and every Sunday members would hug one another and often kisses on the cheek were exchanged. It was half white but the Latin influence was strongest. What I experienced was a church where community mattered and where church members were often in the homes eating and fellowshipping with other members. Community came naturally to the people in the church.

When my family moved to Tennessee, we bought a house in a neighborhood that was about a year old. I noticed that those who had bought homes when the neighborhood first opened spent lots of time together. From what I could gather through conversations with them, none of them were deeply involved in a church. Most did not attend but even those who did are best described as stragglers on the fringe. My wife and I noticed how even those who were not Christians had a desire for some sort of community that they could not get at work, so they found it in their neighborhood.

In the established, predominately white churches I have attended, I have noticed a push for assimilation. For most churches, that means getting people into membership and service, but always within the vision and direction of the church. New members must assimilate to the established order, otherwise they will not fit in well. The church I pastored in Orlando had no assimilation program because it would have been impossible. We would not have had a church left.

I share this story because I believe it illustrates the problem that we have in a lack of community, and how faithful exposition allows us to lay the foundation for healthy community in our local church. The expositor values Scripture because he believes not only that it is the word of God but also because he believes that the Bible is relevant for issues that face modern man. The Scripture that we preach is not a mere ancient religious text. On the contrary, it is the active and living Word of God and it is just as relevant for life today as when it was written. Expository preaching forces the preacher to first expose what the Bible says and then apply it to modern life. There are many issues that most preachers would rather not address but an expositor allows the text to drive his preaching, not the other way around. A preacher who addresses issues in the community could be ignored because he will be seen as preaching his "pet issues." On the other hand, a preacher who avoids anything controversial, especially involving issues of race, could also be ignored by his community because of his failure to speak out. Expository preaching allows the preacher to preach the Word and apply it without apology or excuse, always believing that the Bible will address the issues that his community faces. In other words, expository preaching gives us an avenue to show love to our neighbors.

The Anglican expositor Alec Motyer advises that the preacher needs to keep two things in mind when he preaches. He claims that the first priority is to the truth and the second is to the people. "How will they best hear the truth? How are we to shape and phrase it so that it comes home to them in a way that is palatable, that gains the most receptive hearing, and . . . avoids needless hurt?"[10]

This matters for our preaching because the preached word is what drives the vision of the church. A multi-ethnic church that has been consistently fed the Word through faithful exposition should be able and willing to speak truth to issues about which our neighbors can never seem to agree. In my experience, very few organizations, secular or religious, are voluntarily diverse. This means that, outside of places where we have no choice (work, school, etc.), people mostly stay with those who look and speak and think like they do. A church that is equipped through consistent teaching will be salt and light in a divided and confused world.

Through the faithful exposition of Scripture, the preacher will be able to help the church in its mission to make disciples. My neighbors only have a taste of what real community is. True community is like a feast that God has given to his people and that is only found in the local church. The regular exposition of Scripture is a way to shape the DNA of the church to best serve the community through fulfilling the Great Commission.

---

10. Motyer, *Preaching?*, 65.

Dealing with Racism

Expository preaching also allows us to address issues that are controversial or perhaps divisive. In fact, expository preaching *forces* the preacher to deal with these topics because the text is what drives the sermon. When I began preaching regularly, I read as many books as I could find, hoping that my preaching would improve quickly. I was passionate and wanted to improve so that I could be effective in the pulpit. In all the reading and listening I did, I learned that one of the best benefits of expository for the church is that the pastor cannot skip over uncomfortable texts. If it is in the book he is preaching through he will have to address it in his sermon.

Right now, racism is one of the most controversial topics in the United States. From Black Lives Matter (both the statement and the organization) to police brutality, most people have an opinion and it is, unfortunately, often guided by emotion instead of scriptural truth. The Bible addresses matters of justice and ethnic division, and our preaching needs to expose the truths that God has given to us. Without steady exposition, the preacher can easily fall into preaching only those texts that he prefers or that will not offend anyone. He will neither preach from the minor prophets nor will he address difficult topics. Expository preaching forces the preacher to deal with passages of the Bible that are uncomfortable or those he would rather skip over. A pastor in an all-white church in the South will have a far less difficult time addressing racism as a modern-day application of what the Old Testament prophets proclaimed if all that he's doing is preaching through a book of the Bible. The expositor simply begins with the first verse of a book and does not stop until the conclusion of the book.

Building on that, expository preaching not only forces the preacher to preach about difficult subjects, it first forces him to examine his own life. John Perkins argues that it is too easy for a white person to fail to see that people of color are constantly reminded of their race while he is not. He notes, "The lasting guilt and lingering fears of racism cause people to view those who are different as being almost subhuman, rather than seeing them as children of God created in His image. This is why we talk past one another when racial incidents flare. This is why we ignore other people's stories or perspectives."[11] One would have a very difficult time reading through the Old Testament prophets and not see how their words ought to be applied to the issue of racism and ethnic tension today.

---

11. Perkins, *Dream With Me*, 170.

Preaching without Borders

Author and pastor Daniel Darling has written about issues of race and culture in local churches and he encourages white pastors to preach on race. He contends, "The thrust of God's promise to Abraham and the promises to Israel are His desire to be made known among all nations. And almost every New Testament book embeds its presentation of the gospel with its unifying, reconciling power." He adds that a pastor who devotes himself to expository preaching would have to skip over passages to avoid talking about race.[12]

One criticism of expository preaching is that it is "too white" or "too western." Thabiti Anyabwile believes that expository preaching is "transcultural." He writes, "Cultural assumptions and practices will certainly be present [in any church], but they cannot be allowed to rule. We must cast down everything that exalts itself against the knowledge of God. Everything! Including cultural preference."[13] For a preacher in a multi-ethnic context, this may mean casting down political preferences or even a desire to speak when listening is the best option.

In chapter 4, I addressed how the gospel speaks to social justice and I referenced David Platt's sermon from Amos 5:18–27 that he gave at the 2018 *Together for the Gospel* conference. Platt faced criticism from his sermon, particularly in regards to his perceived misuse of expository preaching. Again, that was discussed in chapter 4. It seems, though, that Platt's sermon hit a nerve with some in predominantly white conservative evangelicalism. Platt's sermon is a quality example of addressing ills in society through expository preaching. Richards and Yang write, "Platt's T4G message wasn't just rhetoric around racial equality and diversity. It's a part of a life-long practice of refining our theology around how God continues to mold culture and ethnicity. It's also an ongoing correction of outdated (and perhaps inadvertently discriminatory) modes of mission."[14] Platt showed that a white preacher can address issues of race from the pulpit through faithful exposition of Scripture.

Faithful exposition will force the preacher to address issues of race and ethnocentrism directly and it will (hopefully) assist the congregation in their understanding of how God's plan is not just for the Jews but for the whole world. In a multi-ethnic congregation, this means that difficult

---

12. Daniel Darling, "Three Reasons White Pastors Need To Start Preaching on Race."

13. Anyabwile, *Reviving the Black Church*, 59.

14. Richards and Yang, "Preaching on Racism."

conversations will be had. The community around the church will feel the blessing because it will (again, hopefully) force the church to examine their witness and service to those not of their own race or background. Expository preaching will, over time, cause a congregation to respond differently when the world is in chaos and ruin. When Christians in a multi-ethnic church are regularly shown how racism and racist concepts and structures stand in opposition to the gospel, believers will be able to respond with a more gospel-centered approach to the strife outside of the church doors.

White pastors who have been raised up and trained in white institutions, for the most part, do not purposely neglect dealing with issues of race. Rather, white pastors mostly lack experience. Pastor and preaching professor David Prince writes, "I believe the reason many white Christians in America fail to see the implications for issues related to racial injustice in the Scripture is the same reason we often read past famine in the Bible without thinking much of it—we have never experienced it."[15] Dan Hyun, a Korean-American pastor in Baltimore echoes this sentiment: "Current events are revealing that faith in Christ itself does not automatically equate to a grasp of the sin of racism. This is particularly true for those where exploring the faith was not required to navigate life as it may have been for people of color." Hyun also notes that unless whites have walked with minorities, "they sometimes don't see racism beyond overt expressions such as those found at White supremacist rallies." Hyun, in preaching to the church and community, adds that he preaches on racism like any other topic and that he doesn't "assume that attendance in a worship service means anything." Hyun also notes that he does not preach about racism for minorities in his church. He writes, "I don't preach about racism to convince minorities in our church that it is a real sin; they already know that. I preach so that they can hear they are not alone."[16]

Gospel Witnesses

I am a firm believer in gospel centrality, meaning that I believe that the issues plaguing us and the world can be answered with the gospel. That does not mean that the gospel will make our lives here and now better in terms of sickness and suffering. We know that Christians often endure hardships worse than those outside of the faith. What gospel centrality means is that

15. Prince, "Preaching About Race."
16. Hyun, "Why I Preach About Racism."

the biggest problem we face (sin), and all of the problems that stem from that, can be answered through the gospel of Jesus Christ. Because of this truth, the gospel is at the center of every Christian's life and if we take Jesus' command in the Great Commission seriously, we must be serious about our witness.

Let's be honest with ourselves: if we were to poll our community, asking them what they thought of our church, what would they say? Many people in my community would know that there is a building on the corner of Wright Road and Gilbert Street, but would they know anything more about my church? Many people would not even know our churches exist. I believe that faithful exposition of God's Word will serve as the catalyst our people need to evangelize and make disciples. Expository preaching forces the preacher to tear down idols in his own life so that he can stand before the congregation on Sunday to tear down the idols of everyone else. It requires the preacher to deal with issues that may be part of his own history or simply the history of the community.

The United States has been engaged in bitter partisan politics for a very long time, certainly much longer than I have been alive. However, it has taken a sharp turn due to the anger and vitriol that has been brought into the light in recent years. In 2016 I watched Christians engage in political arguments on social media. They acted as if the fate of the world and our freedom rested on the results of the presidential election. We hear that every four years now: "This is the most important election of our lifetime." Political engagement should be an encouraging thing for all of us but how often do we count the cost to our testimony?

Suppose I were to place American flags all over my church and, right in front of the pulpit, I put a sign for a particular candidate. If that is too extreme an example, suppose I simply endorse one candidate over another. For most pastors in the United States, that would either bring a pay raise or a letter of termination. But what would happen if I instead stayed silent on the particular candidates and instead continued to preach through books of the Bible, showing that there is a better way forward? What if I were to take stands on what the Bible says rather than what a favored politician says? What if I preached about the sanctity of life, from womb to tomb, showing how God cares about the well-being of his entire creation?

If I used my pulpit to endorse a candidate, I would not only be doing a disservice to my congregation, but I would also be shutting out a large portion of my community. I do not want to pastor a Republican church or Democrat church. In 2016 I saw Christians destroy their testimony because they defended the indefensible. Their friends and neighbors of different political stripes watched that happen. They saw their Christian friends care more about winning an election than anything else and it damaged their Christian witness. It may be many years before we truly feel the severity of the blow to the church that has been caused by politics. This should never happen in a church. Preaching the gospel faithfully through the exposition of Scripture is a safeguard against the creep of politics in the church and it protects our witness to the community by avoiding unnecessarily divisive issues.

Applying the gospel does not just involve politics. Pastor and seminary president Bryan Chappell argues that expository preaching has historically been more common in churches that were suspicious of addressing social issues from the pulpit. He notes,

> The Evangelical church was late to the Civil Rights movement, a secondary voice to Roman Catholicism in sanctity of life efforts, and largely identified with a laissez faire Republicanism in American politics. Something is happening in the area of expository preaching that fits none of these previous stereotypes. Preachers are seeing in the text a certain correction to the North American brand of Evangelicalism that has made a "personal relationship with Jesus" not so much a vital union with the living God, as just another self-enrichment plan for those in a me-first culture. Even in this generation of seminary students the notion that ministry is about sacrifice, mission and leadership for the sake of the body of Christ is a difficult concept for those nurtured on the idea that faith is all about "Jesus and me."

Chappell gives a list of several things that are countering the individualism of modern Evangelicalism, including "Word and deed ministry in the local church for evangelistic outreach, community renewal, and congregational credibility and retention (especially among the young)," and, "greater influence of Asian and African Christianity on North America Evangelicalism helping blinders regarding our individualized faith as a consequence of their cultural emphases on the primacy of the good of the community."[17]

For Chappell, the emphasis in these things that are running contrary to individualism is a return to community. For the Christian, especially in a culture that prizes individualism, community is often neglected. This, however, was not the case in the early church. In Acts 2, we see the fellowship of

---

17. Chappell, "Future of Expository Preaching."

Christians as the gathered church in Jerusalem. These Christians devoted themselves to the teaching of the apostles, fellowship, communion, and prayer. Notice what that devotion to one another did for the gathering:

> And awe came upon every soul, and many wonders and signs were being done through the apostles. And all who believed were together and had all things in common. And they were selling their possessions and belongings and distributing the proceeds to all, as any had need. And day by day, attending the temple together and breaking bread in their homes, they received their food with glad and generous hearts, praising God and having favor with all the people. And the Lord added to their number day by day those who were being saved. (Acts 2:43–47)

It is important to recognize the outcome of their community where the members spent time together, ate together, prayed together, took care of one another, and evangelized together. The impact was not only spiritual growth of the members (though that is certainly a cause for celebration) but it was also in that people were being added to the fellowship "day by day." About this increase in church membership, Polhill contends, "On the receiving end, they experienced the favor of the nonbelieving Jewish community in Jerusalem. God responded to their faith and blessed the young community, adding new converts daily. Indeed, as with the young Jesus, so it was for the growing church—favor with God and favor with humanity."[18] Kistemaker and Hendriksen write, "The phrase does not imply a gradual salvation of the individual believer but rather indicates that the miracle of salvation occurs daily. Today also the Lord continues to add to his church and calls people to be spiritual citizens of the city called Zion."[19]

The church in Jerusalem may not have been as diverse as the church in Galatia at this point but the city was certainly not comprised of only Jews. Jerusalem was a major trade market and was very diverse in terms of religion.[20] The city was also situated at a prominent trade route, making it a hub of activity for locals and those passing through.[21] This, taken with Paul's statement against racial and ethnic division in the church in Galatia ("There is neither Jew nor Greek, there is neither slave nor free, there is no male and female, for you are all one in Christ Jesus."), would naturally

---

18. Polhill, *Acts*, 122.
19. Kistemaker and Hendriksen, *Exposition of the Acts of the Apostles*, 114.
20. Tomasino, "Diversity and Unity in Judaism before Jesus."
21. Hill and Walton, *Survey of the Old Testament*, 46.

Possibilities of Preaching to a Multi-Ethnic Church

lead one to believe that the gospel moved through the early church and out into the diversity of the Jerusalem streets. In addressing John 3:16, Carson observes,

> From this survey it is clear that it is atypical for John to speak of God's love for the *world*, but this truth is therefore made to stand out as all the more wonderful. Jews were familiar with the truth that God loved the children of Israel; here God's love is not restricted by race. Even so, God's love is to be admired not because the world is so big and includes so many people, but because the world is so bad: that is the customary connotation of *kosmos*. The world is so wicked that John elsewhere forbids Christians to love it or anything in it (1 Jn. 2:15–17). There is no contradiction between this prohibition and the fact that God does love it. Christians are not to love the world with the selfish love of participation; God loves the world with the self-less, costly love of redemption.[22]

The gospel that brought the Jerusalem believers new life is the same gospel that has, for two centuries, united Jew and Gentile, man and woman, and free and slave, together as the church. It is no stretch to view the movement of the gospel in Acts as one that moved across the various ethnicities in the city. This evangelism and acts of mercy and service would have certainly been noticed by those outside of the Christian faith. How the church responds to issues that divide the current culture affects how the message of the gospel that we bring is heard and the regular exposition of Scripture is what lays the foundation for this.

Applying the Gospel to Our Lives

Above everything else, a steady diet of expository preaching forces us to confront our own sin and compare it to the perfection of Jesus. Every week I aim to hold up a mirror to my church, showing them what they really are: sinners who have no hope in and of themselves. I also hold up the Bible, showing them that Christ has promised salvation if we turn from our sins and give our lives to him and his work. Engaging in efforts to make our neighborhoods and cities better is noble work and we should lead our churches to support these causes. However, too many churches stop there, thinking that a food pantry or a community service project is missions and

---

22. Carson, *Gospel According to John*, 205.

evangelism. Those play a part in our effort to grow the kingdom of Christ but they must always be guided by the proclaimed gospel truth.

How and what we preach speaks volumes to those in our church and community by showing people what we value. Pastor and author Bryan Loritts claims that in 1 Corinthians 9, we see that the Apostle Paul had an eclectic group of friends. He notes, "Here was a man who had Jewish and Gentile friends (among others). Diversity would be an apt moniker of Paul's tribe, and yet it was not a diversity dipped in the modern ilk of liberalism." Loritts continues,

> After perusing the eclectic nature of his relationships, Paul concludes he does all of this not for popularity, but for the sake of the gospel (1 Cor. 9:23). Scan the shout-outs Paul gives at the end of his letters and what do we find? A list of diverse people. Or revisit why Paul gets thrown in jail for the final time. He's falsely accused of taking his Greek friend Trophimus into the forbidden parts of the temple. Paul had deep Gentile and multiethnic friendships.

Paul's preaching was an outward example of who he was and what he valued. Loritts notes this outward expression of Paul's inward values: "And if I understand Paul correctly, this is Preaching 101. Our effectiveness in the pulpit to reach a multiethnic cohort begins, not just in our study surrounded by a sea of books, but at dinner tables and coffee shops with people who look and see it differently."[23]

There are many ways to preach a sermon, especially with dozens of nationalities represented in the church. I am convinced, however, that the best way for the gospel to be understood by the church and the community is through expository preaching. Will it be challenging to some who are used to more topical sermons? Will it intimidate some who have little experience with doctrinal issues? Will it bother older Christians who have grown up in church? I believe the answer to those questions is an emphatic 'Yes,' but that does not mean that we should avoid letting the Bible speak for itself.

It has been stated in many parts of this chapter, but it bears repeating: the world is watching how Christians respond to matters of race and justice. Too often, our response is fueled more by politics than by Scripture. I am convinced that when the gospel is preached clearly and the entire Word is studied, Christians will see how they should respond to social issues. The Bible is not silent on these things even though we have been at times.

23. Bryan Loritts, "What Is Biblical Preaching?"

Conclusion

Hopefully, this chapter encouraged you to see the positive effects that can happen in a multi-ethnic church and in a community when a preacher commits to expository preaching as his primary means of teaching. As Anyabwile asks, "Can exposition be applied in non-white contexts? Will it preach? Exposition is the only form of preaching that can cross boundaries of time, place, people, and culture. Will it preach? Beloved, nothing else is preaching."[24] In the next chapter, we will see what could happen if expositors fail to adapt to the changes in both our churches and in our communities.

---

24. Anyabwile, *Reviving the Black Church*, 62.

7

What Happens If We Do Not Adapt?

IN THE FIRST SIX chapters I have outlined why preaching the gospel matters and how expositional preaching in a local church is the best way to communicate that to a multi-ethnic church and the surrounding community. In this chapter we will examine some of the effects of not adapting our preaching to the needs and struggles found in a multi-ethnic church family.

Why Not Just Preach the Gospel?

A legitimate question arises whenever a preacher addresses issues of race and racism: why not just preach the gospel? Emerson and Smith's work in *Divided by Faith* is a key text in understanding that evangelicals in the United States do not communicate well when it comes to racism because we are often using the same words while meaning different things. They note that most of the white respondents in their study viewed racism as an individual issue, something that was a result of the sinful state of humanity. In other words, racism is when one person thinks he or she is better than another on the sole basis of their skin color or ethnicity. On the other hand, black Christians view the problem of racism as structural or institutional. Emerson and Smith write, "All this helps us understand why two-thirds of white Americans (and evangelicals) believe conditions for blacks are improving, while just one-third of African Americans believe that." This is the

What Happens If We Do Not Adapt?

reason why discussions about race are difficult because the understanding of racism is so different.[1]

There are some well-known preachers who contend that our duty is to preach the Word of God and nothing more. Some have said that social justice is not only not part of the gospel, but also actually a hindrance to the gospel.[2] This critique is valid if the preacher is preaching that social justice has salvific power or that it is part of the gospel. While that may be true of some, that is not the definition or understanding of expository preaching used in this research. Instead, I have attempted to show that dealing with social justice is an effect of faithful exposition.

Being aware of what matters to our community is important because public opinion about what matters has shifted. In the 1950s, rock 'n' roll was a popular target for preachers.[3] In the era before and during prohibition, preachers like Billy Sunday would use their pulpits to campaign against the consumption of alcohol.[4] Preaching about rock 'n' roll and drinking seem like ancient history but, no matter how one may feel about these issues from a Christian perspective, they did address issues that were important for those eras. A cynical view, though certainly truthful in some respects, could attribute the preaching focus on these issues to giving listeners what they wanted but there is no doubt that much of the preaching was intended to effect some societal change.

While sermons against rock 'n' roll and alcohol are, in large part, a relic of the past, preachers must be able to apply the gospel to modern concerns. A 2019 Barna Group study of eighteen to thirty-five-year-olds showed that racism is one of the most pressing concerns, along with corruption, climate change, pollution, and extreme poverty.[5] In other words, for a preacher to be effective to young people, he must be able to show how the Bible speaks to issues that are important to them. To put it in terms of this research, for a preacher to be effective in his community, he must be willing to adapt.

As previously stated, expository preaching should force the preacher to address these issues. When asked whether we should preach the gospel or justice, our answer should emphatically be: both! As one South African minister wrote:

1. Emerson and Smith, *Divided By Faith*, 88.
2. John MacArthur, "Social Justice and the Gospel, Part 1."
3. Randall J. Stephens, "'Where Else Did They Copy Their Styles.'"
4. John Fea, "'Town That Billy Sunday Could Not Shut Down."
5. "18-35-Year-Olds Rate the Church's Reputation for Justice."

> Across Africa we've witnessed slavery, colonialism and Apartheid. These were advocated for and approved by many Christians because the church kept silent, because of their skewed theology of justice and our mission in the world. We've also seen a departure from the gospel with the emergence of the social gospel because other Christians were not immersed and rooted in the foundational doctrines of the gospel. We need to guard ourselves and the church from these two extremes. But praise God that we've seen, and in fact have biblical evidence of, faithful preachers who consistently and faithfully proclaimed both justice and justification by faith.[6]

Preaching the good news of Jesus saving sinners leaves us no other option than to deal with our own sin and the sin that we see around us. The gospel saves us from the wrath of God and it also causes us to live and behave differently. It causes us to speak up for the unborn and for the downtrodden, the marginalized, and the oppressed.[7]

Contextualization is essential for the preacher. Throughout church history there have been heresies and shallow doctrine taught under the guise of faithful teaching. Those false teachers have exchanged the freedom and liberty that comes from the gospel for something that does not accomplish anything beyond earthly comfort. Pastor Ryan Huguley warns of this:

> The fear is that if we *contextualize* the message, we will somehow *compromise* it. This criticism assumes we may be attempting to soften biblical imperatives. If we're pulling proverbial punches for fear of offending modern ears, we're not contextualizing—we're stripping the message of its truth and power. When done correctly, though, contextualization does not compromise. In contextualizing, we simply labor to make the original meaning of the ancient text clearer to modern ears. Even Jesus contextualized when He drew images from first-century agrarian settings to teach His parables. When Jesus spoke of farmers (Matt. 13:3–9), shepherds (John 10), and vineyards (Matt. 20:1–16), he was contextualizing. He was using everyday references to convey eternal truths. That is our task as well. At no point are we to distort or dumb down the text, but we are to lead our listeners back into its historical setting and meaning by using language, imagery, and ideas that people can understand.[8]

---

6. David Cloete, "False Rivalry."
7. Ps 33:5; Prov 31:8–9; Micah 6:8; Heb 13:3
8. Huguley, *8 Hours or Less*, 28.

What Happens If We Do Not Adapt?

As it has been mentioned previously, contextualization is taking the truth of Scripture and using terms and illustrations from the culture in which we live and then applying the text of the Bible to the problems that our listeners face. Our aim is to preach the gospel, but our effectiveness will be hindered if we fail to speak the "language" of the people.

Dangers of Not Adapting our Preaching

A faithful preacher should have a desire to reach more people for the gospel, but not every preacher is willing or equipped to preach effectively across ethnic lines. There are serious dangers that will limit our reach if we do not adapt our preaching to meet the needs of those in our congregation of a different ethnicity or culture. This list is not every problem that could arise in the future, but it is a sampling of some common issues that are likely to happen if the preacher does not accurately recognize, assess, and adjust his preaching.

Barriers Will Block Us

I have often said to my church that I want to remove all the unnecessary barriers from our church life and church service that will prevent someone from hearing the gospel, responding to it, and joining our church. Every church has barriers of some kind and every preacher will face a variety of barriers in their regular preaching of the Word. The first common barrier involves language. This is not only referencing different languages but how our words are understood, even when preacher and listener share the same tongue. Jensen and Grimmond are aware of the need in the local church to remove these impediments of gospel growth. They write, "Preachers should try as much as possible to understand the culture of their audience and to preach in a way that is appropriate. This will extend from the kind of humour we employ (or choose not to employ) to the kind of clothing that we choose to wear. It is all part of breaking down the barriers that might keep our listeners from hearing what is said."[9]

A multi-ethnic church in the United States may be comprised of all English speakers but there is likely a chasm in how people hear and interpret what is being said. This is most common in illustrations that a preacher

---

9. Jensen and Grimmond, *Archer and the Arrow*, 90.

employs. A pastor of a church in rural Maine will likely not be able to effectively use the same illustrations as a pastor in Los Angeles or San Francisco. Henry Mitchell contends:

> Another imaginative aspect of Black preaching is the choice of illustrations—gripping modern parallels to the biblical text. In the process of making the point clear, the Black experience is lifted up and celebrated, identity is enhanced, and the hearer enters vicariously into the story, making it his or her own personal story. It is just as destructive to the religious growth of Black people to use illustrations from White middle-class life as it is destructive to Black children's reading skills to have Black children reading only from White middle-class 'Dick and Jane' books.[10]

A preacher in a diverse church will need to be skillful in using language that people understand. A failure to do so will likely mean a failure to communicate well and people will stop listening.

Another barrier is style. The easiest way to ensure that people will not pay attention to our preaching is by being boring. A sermon cannot be delivered like a budget presentation in a conference. Atkinson notes, "If you sound bored with your own subject matter, the audience can hardly be expected to feel any differently about it. This is why, of all the emotions that can be conveyed through intonation, enthusiasm must surely be the most important one of all."[11] The preacher needs to know how his audience speaks and hears. He needs to be aware of the way he frames sentences and how he emphasizes words because his job is to keep his listeners' attention so that nothing comes between them and the gospel.

The last barrier is that our differences in understanding theology can lead to people segregating themselves. DeYoung, et al., write that African Americans hold to more traditional theological views than do mainline Protestant whites while, at the same time, holding more progressive views than conservative evangelicals. This creates a kind of homelessness that often results in black Christians staying part of black churches rather than leaving their church communities to join in majority white congregations. They write that black Christians "in white churches will either be a theological or political mismatch for the rest of the congregation."[12] The expositor must seek

---

10. Mitchell, *Black Preaching*, 66–67.
11. Atkinson, *Lend Me Your Ears*, 61.
12. DeYoung, et al., *United by Faith*, 109–10.

What Happens If We Do Not Adapt?

to set aside those non-essential, non-convictional aspects of his preaching so that more people will hear how the gospel can change their lives.

Bridges Will Be Burned

The second danger is that bridges will be burned. Preaching is so much more than relaying information from the speaker to the listener. Effective preaching that makes an impact on the lives of the congregation comes when the preacher knows the stories and struggles of the people. Robert Smith argues:

> The moral conscience of doctrine makes arrangements for preaching to meet at the intersection of the vertical relationship between God and humans and the horizontal relationship between humans and humans. This moral conscience of doctrine insists that preachers be acquainted not only with the streets of gold in heaven but also with the streets of gloom in the ghetto. It unites the pulpit and the pavement, the sanctuary and the street, Bethlehem and Birmingham, the New Jerusalem and New Jersey.[13]

Not knowing the needs of the people in their unique setting is a recipe for problems for the preacher. Kim notes that preaching involves three staples: hermeneutics, humans, and homiletics. The preacher must be able to understand God's Word, the listeners, and how to communicate effectively, especially when it's done across ethnic or racial divides.[14]

What I mean when I refer to bridges being burned is that it takes time for the preacher to earn credibility with his congregation. Many sermons will be preached, and many interactions will be had before the congregation chooses to follow the pastor's leadership.[15] Preachers are building bridges between the ancient world and today, and they are doing the same within their own congregations—between people of different cultural backgrounds and experiences. The preacher must navigate these often-difficult situations to prevent burning bridges and ensure a future with the people God has called him to shepherd.

---

13. Smith, *Doctrine That Dances*, 19.

14. Kim, *Preaching with Cultural Intelligence*, xiv.

15. Thom Rainer, "Why It Takes Five to Seven Years to Become the Pastor of a Church."

We Will Give in to Fear and Rely on Our Own Strength

The third danger of not adapting is that we will give in to fear and thus rely on our own strength. In all parts of our lives, fear is a factor in our decision making. In preaching, fear can drive us to avoid addressing topics and passages that the congregation and community need to hear. Fear leads us to avoid things like racism, ethnocentrism, and Christian nationalism. Nieman and Rogers write:

> Had not the first believers been effective at preaching amid those who were different from themselves, the church would not have endured beyond that first generation. Moreover, had not every subsequent generation of believers taken up that same challenge anew in its own place and time, then the gospel itself would be but a faint voice on the horizon of many competing religious claims.[16]

Nieman and Rogers follow up that thought by later saying, "The problem for us today, however, is not this long history of cultural diversity itself, but that we have chosen to fear rather than welcome it."[17]

Fear in our preaching will naturally lead us to rely on our own strength. So many times, throughout Scripture, we are warned about relying on ourselves. Proverbs 3:5 says, "Trust in the Lord with all your heart, and do not lean on your own understanding." Merida warns against putting trust in our own strength when he claims:

> We must be mindful of *our own human limitations*. It is easy for the eloquent pastor to preach in the flesh. Paul reminded the Corinthians that his preaching was done "with a demonstration of the Spirit and power" (1 Cor 2:4). While Paul did employ rhetorical elements in his preaching (e.g., Acts 17:16–34), and was himself a highly educated man, he still understood that his ultimate hope was in the powerful work of the Spirit. He actually reveled in these weaknesses (1 Cor 2:3). Regardless of our wit and charisma, like Paul, we are "clay pots" (2 Cor 4:7). We must never lose the *fear* of preaching God's Word (1 Cor 2:2), and we must never lose the feeling of *powerlessness* apart from God's Spirit. A failure to experience these two realities is a glaring reminder of our sickening pride. We are in over our head. Much is at stake. May we preach with a holy fear and a sincere desperation. Like Paul, we must

---

16. Nieman and Rogers, *Preaching to Every Pew*, 1.
17. Nieman and Rogers, *Preaching to Every Pew*, 8.

desperately desire to see God transform hearts, instead of desiring to captivate a crowd.[18]

Arturo Azurdia warns the preacher that he cannot be self-sufficient because he relies on the testimony of God. He writes, "To then attempt a proclamation of that message in a manner that relies upon methods reflecting the wizardry of men is to eviscerate the gospel of its own content." The cross does not only become the substance of our preaching, it tells us how to preach, specifically that it is not the preacher or his words that bring change, but rather Christ and Christ alone.[19]

Giving in to fear means that we trust ourselves rather than the power of the Holy Spirit. Orrick, et al., write that a preacher will spend hours preparing his sermon but only giving "fleeting moments" to seek the power of the Holy Spirit. They write, "As a result, our preaching is very different than the preaching of the New Testament authors. It is far too often orthodox but ineffective, polished but powerless. We may say the right words, but neither we nor our hearers are experiencing God in our preaching."[20] They later write that the Spirit-filled preacher is "one who has tasted and seen in the Word that the Lord is good . . . His sermons are not just a lecture, but a lecture and a field trip rolled into one: a lecture in that they teach the subject matter clearly, and a field trip in that the subject matter is experienced."[21]

As shown in previous chapters, there is strong biblical evidence that diversity in the church is not only helpful, but it is preferred. Certainly, a community that is monoethnic cannot have a diverse congregation but the number of churches that match the diversity of their respective communities is lacking. There is a disconnect happening in churches that are not as diverse as their community, whether it be historical (as with many churches in formerly segregated communities) or because of preference. Either way, it seems that fear of different races and ethnicities plays a role in this lack of diverse congregations.[22]

---

18. Merida, *Christ-Centered Expositor*, 89.
19. Azurdia III, *Spirit Empowered Preaching*, 89.
20. Orrick, Payne, and Fullerton, *Encountering God*, 90.
21. Orrick, Payne, and Fullerton, *Encountering God*, 91–92.
22. Jones, "Racism among White Christians Is Higher than among the Nonreligious."

Preaching without Borders

We Will Lose Our Missional Edge

The fourth danger of not adapting is that we will lose our missional edge. Though there are a variety of definitions of the term *missional*, for this work I define it by what Jesus said is Matt 28:19–20: "Go therefore and make disciples of all nations, baptizing them in the name of the Father and of the Son and of the Holy Spirit, teaching them to observe all that I have commanded you." In other words, being missional is living in such a way that evangelism and discipleship moves from being an activity to a way of life. Regarding this concept of missional living in Matthew 28, Merida concludes:

> We should not forget that preaching has a missional edge to it. We speak to different audiences in an attempt to make disciples of "all nations" (*pana ta ethne*, Matt 28:18–20). Of course, in today's global world, contextualization is needed across the street as much as it is needed across the seas. We should learn, like Paul, how to speak with cultural sensitivity to different groups of people in order that we may win some to Christ (1 Cor 9:23). When Paul spoke to the Jewish audience, he began with Scriptures, and when he spoke to the Greeks, he referenced their philosophers. With both audiences, he preached the resurrected Christ (Acts 17:3–5, 22–34).[23]

Having a "missional edge" is essential to the preacher in a multi-ethnic church and community because his work is, in many ways, similar to what a missionary will face when he or she steps onto foreign soil. Churches in diverse communities cannot afford to ignore the trends and changes in demographics. The United States Census Bureau projects that by 2030, immigration will overtake natural births as the primary driver of population growth.[24] In other words, the United States is becoming more of a international mission field in our own backyard.

When our preaching does not adapt to the culture in which God has placed us, we will have a mission with no "edge." Our preaching may contain excellent exegesis and a superb handling of the original languages, but it will not make a difference in the life of the congregation and community without adapting to the surrounding culture. Helm adds that Paul gives the example to us regarding how to read the Bible and how that extends to our preaching. He notes:

---

23. Merida, *Christ-Centered Expositor*, 217–18.
24. Vespa, Medina, and Manning, "Demographic Turning Points for the United States."

What Happens If We Do Not Adapt?

> First, the skills of reasoning, proving, and persuading marked Paul's approach when preaching Christ from all the Scriptures. Each of these terms has a rich background in Hellenistic moral philosophy and demonstrates a rigorous, thoughtful practice. Second, he employed these tools in diverse contexts—in the synagogue and the marketplace, in the presence of both Jews and Greeks. There were no shortcuts for one audience or another. Third, Paul found ways to preach this same gospel in settings where no biblical knowledge could be assumed. There is a way of preaching to people who lack a biblical background and vocabulary.[25]

Paul had what Merida would call a "missional edge." He preached to people who had no religious background, so he had to adjust his preaching to better communicate with those he encountered.

Jensen and Grimmond rightly note that the preacher puts himself in a much better position to be faithful and effective when he builds his preaching around what the Bible says, not what sociological research tells us. They write, "The Bible grants us the spiritual insight to see the half-hearted, self-obsessed, self-deceived, God-rejecting, neighbor-coveting hearts of ourselves and our hearers. And the Scriptures also provide us with the only possible solution—the gospel of Jesus."[26] Every faithful preacher should be nodding in agreement, but how will the preacher be able to present the gospel in the language of the people without sociology? Different people have different lenses through which they see their need for the gospel. Jensen and Grimmond seem to agree with this assessment only a page later when they write, "Knowing the gospel is therefore not an excuse for poor observation skills or lack of wisdom."[27]

In his book, *Fool's Talk: Recovering the Art of Christian Persuasion*, Os Guinness argues that Christians cannot approach evangelism the same way for different people. The world is simply too diverse, and people think much too differently to keep a "one size fits all" method of evangelism. He writes:

> No single method will ever fit everyone because every single person is different, and every method—even the best—will miss someone. There is no question that the Four Spiritual Laws have been remarkably fruitful as a way of evangelism, but they are not good for everyone. The first law, "God loves you and offers a wonderful plan for your life," may be perfect for people who believe

25. Helm, *Expositional Preaching*, 63.
26. Jensen and Grimmond, *Archer and the Arrow*, 95.
27. Jensen and Grimmond, *Archer and the Arrow*, 96.

even vaguely in God, and it even speaks to an atheist who is beginning to search for "something more." But it is meaningless and water off a duck's back for an atheist satisfied with his atheism. Worse, to a hostile atheist, mention of God at the start of the conversation is like a red rag to a bull, and invites a snort and a pawing of the ground. As we need to remind ourselves again and again, and then again, *Jesus never spoke to two people the same way, and neither should we. Every single person is unique and individual and deserves an approach that respects that uniqueness.*[28]

The preacher who fails to adapt his preaching to his audience will fail to fully connect with them and this is especially true when the preaching is being delivered to a diverse, multi-ethnic congregation.

Anticipating Tension

Those dangers of not adapting are not easy things to correct. Addressing things that the Bible says, particularly issues like racism, immigration, and other sensitive topics, will often create difficulties for the preacher. This is true even in the most diverse congregations. The preacher must be prepared for the tension that will come when he applies the Bible to modern life and problems. Edward Gilbreath recognizes this tension when he argues:

> From the first-century believers to the Protestant Reformation to the civil rights movement, the church's role has been defined by tension and paradox—to be wise as serpents and gentle as doves, to lose your life to find it, to be in the world but not of it. The Christian life is a precarious balance between heaven and earth, Christ and culture, spirit and flesh. And evangelicalism was born out of that tension. Throw race into the mix and things get even trickier.[29]

Cultures clashing in a church where people from different ethnicities and backgrounds make up the congregation is not merely a possibility. It will happen and pastors must be aware of this and prepared for the conflicts that will arise.

Tension over issues of race and how preachers are to handle sensitive topics in the pulpit is not confined to one denomination or theological perspective. Riverside Church in New York City is an example of tension arising in liberal/progressive congregations. The church is known for its

28. Guinness, *Fool's Talk*, 33.
29. Gilbreath, *Reconciliation Blues*, 40.

What Happens If We Do Not Adapt?

progressive political activism started by its first pastor, Harry Emerson Fosdick, and its benefactor, John D. Rockefeller, Jr. In 1989, after more than sixty years in existence, Riverside called its first black pastor, James Forbes. Forbes' trial sermon, delivered in early 1989, was "electrifying" and "brought the congregation joyously to its feet," but that joy would not last long.[30] DeYoung, et al., note that the tension was apparent early in Forbes' preaching ministry:

> Although Forbes was welcomed enthusiastically by most of the congregation, the church has had to come to terms with racial and cultural differences. For example, Forbes preaches in the oral tradition, which is typical in African American churches. Not only are sermons in the oral tradition longer than those in predominantly white congregations, but they also elicit a response from the congregation. When Forbes began preaching, some members were uncomfortable with the "Amens" and the clapping during the sermons. The church even held meetings about the matter, during which white members asked their pastor to discourage people from responding during his sermons. They noted that the responses made them feel like they were at a "show" and prevented them from hearing the sermon itself. This is an example of the clashes and misunderstandings that can occur within a multiracial congregation.[31]

On the more conservative side of the theological spectrum, Zack Eswine describes the tension that comes in diverse church cultures. He notes:

> Similar is the fact that a watch not only tells time but also influences moral judgment. In a white cultural context, if a preacher's sermon goes long, people in the congregation and especially in the nursery may actually judge the preacher's moral character. They find themselves saying things like, "He doesn't care about our children," or "He doesn't respect us."
>
> In contrast, in an African American setting, if one preaches too short, nursery workers and congregational members may likewise challenge the preacher's character for opposite reasons: "Doesn't he care about our children? We need the Word." "Is he more concerned about time than with the things of God?" Technological assumptions shape the thinking of a place.[32]

---

30. Goldman, "Members Elect A New Pastor At Riverside."
31. DeYoung, et al., *United by Faith*, 81.
32. Eswine, *Preaching to a Post-Everything World*, 186–87.

The preacher stands in an "awkward and uncomfortable" position, "striving to love and affirm the congregation while, at the same time, prodding and stretching it toward a larger worldview and greater faithfulness to its own gospel."[33]

A tension that is unique to white pastors in the United States is the "normalization of whiteness." In other words, privilege. Very few words are as angering to white people as the term *privilege* who, by in large, do not understand or accept the concept of white privilege.[34] While privilege is indeed a loaded word and it has many possible definitions Pastor Daniel Hill defines the term as "the ability to walk away." He contends:

> This is one of the essential truths we as white people need to remember (or become aware of, if it's new) as we contend with the normalization of whiteness. When the journey begins to feel like any combination of scary, confusing, disorienting, or even painful, we have a privilege that people of color do not: we can walk away; we can go back to 'normal,' if we choose.[35]

Privilege does not necessarily mean money or special rights given by the government, though it can certainly contain both. Having "the ability to walk away" contains within it the ability to move as one pleases, as shown in the case of Rachel Dolezal. A white woman, Dolezal posed as a black woman, even becoming a chapter president of the National Association for the Advancement of Colored People (NAACP) and a professor of Africana Studies. When it became public that she was not black, her supporters claimed that she could identify however she chose to identify. Her detractors said that for Dolezal to claim to be able to "opt in" to black culture and identity, it would suggest that black people can somehow "opt out." Errin Whack, a journalist, notes:

> Being black is not a lifestyle or a choice. One can no more choose to be black than we can choose our age or height. Unlike my gender identity, which I could alter by cutting my hair and wearing different clothes, asking people to address me with a male pronoun or even undergoing gender reassignment surgery, I cannot change the color of my skin, the trails of my ancestors or the way that a

---

33. Tisdale, *Preaching as Local Theology and Folk Art*, 53.
34. "Expert: Data Shows Many Whites Don't Connect Privilege To Race."
35. Hill, *White Awake*, 38.

What Happens If We Do Not Adapt?

majority-white country still very much invested in the concept of racial identity will always perceive me.[36]

The Dolezal case was unique and received extensive press coverage but the point for preachers is that the tension exists. Attempting to connect with the audience by addressing certain social ills through the gospel while not inadvertently (or purposely, unfortunately) creating a caricature is not an exact science. What this means is that there will often be a sense of tension in multi-ethnic churches between preacher and congregation.

Conclusion

The dangers of not adapting our preaching are clear. A balance needs to be struck between holding fast to the traditions of the past and adapting or contextualizing our preaching to speak to issues that people today face. In the next chapter I will give some practical suggestions for the preacher who desires to make the changes to his preaching in order to be more effective in reaching the nations in his own backyard.

---

36. Whack, "Choosing to Be Black Is the Epitome of White Privilege."

8

What Preachers Can Do

To ASK WHAT PREACHERS can do to preach in such a way that the gospel is heard and understood is a huge question that cannot be entirely addressed in one volume. As previously mentioned, this work should serve as a primer of sorts. It is a challenge to examine what the Bible says and what the culture needs in terms of gospel proclamation through the preaching of the Word. In this chapter, I hope to help the reader take the next step forward in their journey as a preacher. This involves four areas of study: yourself, your church, your community, and God. At first glance, these categories of study sound simplistic but all the practical wisdom and advice that we have seen throughout this book can be summarized into one of these categories.

Studying these four categories can produce wisdom that will guide pastors. Our study as heralds of God's Word does not stop when we graduate seminary or finish an ordination process. It is my hope that the reader views this list as a summary of all that has been said up to this point.

Study Yourself

One may read this chapter and question the order of advice given. After all, it is far more important to study who God is and what God does than to study ourselves, is it not? Of course, our study of God is the most important thing that we can do; however, our understanding of God and how he works is colored by the knowledge of our own strengths and weaknesses. Often, though, we are unaware at what we are good at and what we are not. Tom Nichols argues:

> The more specific reason that unskilled or incompetent people overestimate their abilities far more than others is because they lack a key skill called 'metacognition.' This is the ability to know when you're not good at something by stepping back, looking at what you're doing, and then realizing that you're doing it wrong. Good singers know when they've hit a sour note; good directors know when a scene in a play isn't working; good marketers know when an ad campaign is going to be a flop. Their less competent counterparts, by comparison, have no such ability. They think they're doing a great job.[1]

Experts—something we hope to become—cannot get to an "expert" level without first having a clear understanding of their own skills and weaknesses. To Nichols, this is a dividing line between competence and incompetence.

It is my experience that the most overlooked aspect of preaching and pastoral ministry is a pastor's failure to be self-aware. 1 Timothy 4:16 says, "Keep a close watch on yourself and on the teaching. Persist in this, for by so doing you will save both yourself and your hearers." Every person who steps behind the pulpit must keep a close watch on himself and that only happens when we know well who we are. Abraham Booth, an eighteenth-century pastor in London, delivered a sermon from this text where he said, "Take heed to yourself, respecting the motives by which you are influenced in all your endeavors to obtain useful knowledge. For if you read and study, chiefly that you may cut a respectable figure in the pulpit; or to obtain and increase popular applause; the motive is carnal, base, and unworthy a man of God."[2]

Knowing oneself does not end with merely knowing skills and weaknesses. Knowing ourselves goes to the deepest, darkest places in our own hearts. In the first chapter of his *Institutes of the Christian Religion*, John Calvin writes, "Our wisdom, in so far as it ought to be deemed true and solid Wisdom, consists almost entirely of two parts: the knowledge of God and of ourselves."[3] In other words, we cannot know ourselves if we do not know God. Consider that the opposite is also true: we cannot fully grasp

---

1. Nichols, *Death of Expertise*, 45.
2. Booth, "Pastoral Cautions," 34.
3. John Calvin, *Institutes of the Christian Religion*, 37.

the goodness of God and the glory of his grace unless we understand our pitiful sinfulness. According to Robert Smith:

> The preacher who handles the Word must first be touched by that same Word. Doctrinal preaching has an impact within both the cognitive and the emotive sectors. Preaching that leaves the cognitive untouched produces hearers who may leave the sanctuary feeling better but without having been helped by the deep doctrinal truths of the Scriptures. Classical rhetoricians attempted to be holistic in the speech act: enlighten the mind, touch the heart, and move the will. Preaching that avoids head engagement will lead to blindness, and preaching that ignores heart engagement—the emotive realm of the believer's existence—does so at the cost of boredom and dullness, which prevents the result of an engaged hearing for a transformed life.[4]

The task of the preacher is to constantly remind himself of his own sinfulness so that the glory of God shines through in his life and his preaching.

The preacher is called to care for the souls of those God has entrusted to him. As Harold Senkbeil concludes in *The Care of Souls: Cultivating a Pastor's Heart*, a pastor/preacher should view his vocation in the same way a doctor views his own. A medical doctor cares for the body while a spiritual doctor (pastor/preacher) cares for the soul. He notes, "Two things are indispensable for the job description of one who serves as a spiritual physician: being attentive and being intentional. Faithful diagnosis and cure include both."[5] The preacher is to diagnose and work to heal the spiritual infirmities of those under his care. He cannot do that well if he does not know himself and the gospel well.

A practical way to study yourself is by examining your own cultural and ethnic history. *What is it that leads me to believe this or that about a certain issue?* We are influenced by our cultural and familial experience more than many of us realize. That also includes the values and history that have been passed down through generations. Another way to improve our understanding of who we are is by asking others about our blind spots, specifically in relation to culture, ethnicity, and race. I was raised in a white, middle-class family and we lived in a mostly white neighborhood and went to mostly white schools. I was in my thirties before my views about race were challenged by a Christian brother of color. My friend guided me

---

4. Smith, *Doctrine That Dances*, 2.
5. Senkbeil, *Care of Souls*, 99.

through a long process of self-examination and some difficult times where I had to break down how I saw the world. It was not easy but it was pivotal in shaping me as a preacher.

Study Your Church

The second piece of advice given here is that you must study your church. It is much easier to study the Bible and prepare and deliver a sermon in isolation from the community in which one lives. A faithful preacher, however, cannot be separated from the sheep that he is called to shepherd. Otis Moss claims:

> There are some people in your congregation, as my friend, D. Daryl Griffin says, who are head folk. They want something that is broken down in a very didactic way. Then there are some heart folk; you got to tell some stories. Then there are some gut folk. They want you to move from the page. But these people are all in the same sanctuary, which means you have to be a student of the people in your sanctuary. You must understand, so you cannot be married to one way of communication, because you may not reach them with that form of communication. Or you may have to bring someone in who communicates in a different way.[6]

The preacher faces the weekly challenge to know the Word but also to preach in such a way that every person in the congregation can grow from it. This certainly includes those of a different ethnicity or cultural background from the pastor but also includes different learning styles, disabilities, and educational experience.

Orrick, Payne, and Fullerton, use the example of Paul in Corinth to show how the preacher must study the congregation well. They write:

> While in Corinth, Paul deliberately chose a style of delivery that would enhance the message of salvation through faith alone in Christ alone. In determining his methodology, Paul considered the culture of Corinth and the characteristics of his hearers. Then, from a variety of rhetorical options, he chose the one that he believed was best suited for that particular setting and that particular group of people. This is a process that all effective preachers must go through. Virtually all effective preachers and teachers know the culture of their hearers and the unique characteristics

---

6. Moss III, *Blue Note Preaching in a Post-Soul World*, 57.

of the particular congregation that will be in front of them when it comes time to preach. This enables the preacher accurately to predict how the congregation will receive or react to everything that is said. Good preachers and teachers know human nature, and they work hard to customize their delivery to their audience. Sometimes this customization means that the preacher leaves out certain oratorical or poetic flourishes of which he is capable, leaving them out because they would be a distraction. This is what Paul did at Corinth. Other times, a preacher must work hard to improve his grammar or his speaking skills because his poor delivery is a distraction for his audience.[7]

The preacher, according to Robert Smith, has two obligations. He must be faithful to the text, and he must be sensitive to the hearers.[8] A preacher who does not recognize that each church is different will quickly find himself being tuned out by those in the congregation.

Preachers must become experts in their field—the local church. Tisdale charges that preachers need to become "amateur ethnographers—skilled in observing and in thickly describing the subcultural signs and symbols of the congregations they serve."[9] She says that each preacher must ask himself:

> What is distinctive about a particular congregation's subcultural identity? How does one go about reading the signs and symbols of congregational life in order to discern congregational worldview, values, and ethos? Are there any paradigms by which a local pastor can distinguish between his or her own subcultural understandings and those of the congregation?[10]

Becoming an expert in anything takes both time and hard work, but the payoff is a more fruitful ministry where the church will grow in the faith. McQuoid asserts that preaching is pastoral ministry in the sense that our sermons will fall flat if we are unable to connect the Bible with the daily lives of those in the church:

> If we want to apply the Word of God to peoples' lives, we need to know the people we are preaching to and the issues that will be

---

7. Orrick, Payne, and Fullerton, *Encountering God Through Expository Preaching*, 113–14.

8. Smith, *Doctrine That Dances*, 22.

9. Tisdale, *Preaching as Local Theology and Folk Art*, 60.

10. Tisdale, *Preaching as Local Theology and Folk Art*, 18.

relevant to them. It will not do just to have a good knowledge of the Bible and the principles of biblical interpretation. Neither is it sufficient to spend all our time locked in the study doing endless biblical exegesis. We need to be out talking to people and discovering where they are at in their relationship with God, so that our sermons can minister to their needs. In this sense preaching and pastoral work go together and complement each other.[11]

As stated previously in this book, the preacher must have a firm understanding of his congregation if his preaching is to be effective. In sports, a coach will sometimes tell his players to "keep their head on a swivel," meaning that there are moments that demand more attention than others. In a multi-ethnic church, the pastor must always "have his head on a swivel," because good communication is essential for his effectiveness, and good communication must begin with knowing one's audience. Koessler claims:

> Even when the audience's native language is the same as ours, preaching is always an exercise in translation. We are bound by the ideas of the biblical text when we preach, but we are also constrained by the culture and life situation of those who hear us. As we put the ideas of the biblical text on display, we draw out specific implications for a specific audience. If we are to fulfill our responsibility as God's messengers, we must deliver his message in language that our listeners can understand.
> It is tempting to assign each of these forces its own pole in the sermon—to say, for example, that the text governs exegesis and hermeneutics while the audience controls specific application and the mode of proclamation. It is true that the biblical author and the life situation of the original audience dominate the exegetical and hermeneutical phases of the sermon. Yet even in these early stages, those who will be listening to us are never far from view. Our awareness of the audience during the exegetical process affects the angle of vision we take on the text, creating a kind of filter that determines which exegetical and hermeneutical data we will select for emphasis.[12]

Having an awareness of one's congregation means that the process of creating a sermon will take into account the needs of everyone in the church. The more diverse a church, the more difficult the task will be for the preacher.

---

11. McQuoid, *Beginner's Guide to Expository Preaching*, 116.
12. Koessler, *Folly, Grace, and Power*, 86–87.

What does this look like in the normal rhythms of pastoral ministry? First, we must be willing to get to know the sheep (John 10:14–15, 27). What I mean is that while we may prefer to sit in our study with our books and favorite dead theologians, we will never be able to connect well with the church if that is all that we do. Spending significant time with our church members is beneficial to them in that it allows us to hear their stories. It is also beneficial to us as it shows our people that we actually care about them and think about them in our sermon preparation. Second, we must build margin into our schedules, so that we have availability to be with members of our congregation. We can never expect the church to work around our busy schedule so we must adapt to their schedules. Third, we should take a genuine interest in their lives, asking questions about their concerns, hopes, dreams, and hurts. This means asking questions that will allow conversations to go deeper. An effective preacher will make time spent with the congregation an important part of his sermon preparation. According to Vines and Shaddix, "The preacher . . . must approach every sermon with a particular audience in mind. This demand means that he study the people and the context every time he prepares a sermon. He is bringing God's message to a particular group of people, and real preaching involves a consideration of that group's character and circumstances."[13]

The pastor/preacher should begin to study his church by simply paying attention to who is in the congregation. Kim writes:

> Imagine yourself preaching to listeners of the opposite gender only. How would you feel? Would your sermon preparation change in any noticeable way? Would you alter your content, delivery style, language, facial expressions, tone, illustrations, or applications? Preaching to the other gender poses many questions as we think more intentionally about our listeners.[14]

This statement is helpful and should be applied to each different demographic in our congregation. How much improvement would we see on Sunday morning if, during the week prior, we considered the different cultures and backgrounds of those in our church?

If you have been at your church for any length of time, you will likely have an adequate understanding of who your church is and what makes the congregation unique. What I have found, though, is that we must go deeper. Small-talk and surface level conversations do not allow us to adequately

---

13. Vines and Shaddix, *Power in the Pulpit*, 26.
14. Kim, *Preaching with Cultural Intelligence*, 127.

hear what people really think. A responsibility of the pastor is to know the sheep so we must make it a high priority to visit with each member of our church and listen to them, paying attention to what they say and what they do not say. Sometimes, however, respect for those in leadership will limit what people say to the pastor. Here, a demographic study of the congregation would be a helpful place to start. This can be accomplished through a created survey by the church or by using an outside resource, like "Church Answers," a ministry led by Dr. Thom Rainer, the former president of Lifeway Christian Resources. Doing this congregational survey will allow the pastor to see what people really think, especially from people who come from cultures that do not question leadership.

Study Your Community

A third piece of advice is that you must study your community. So far, we have expanded outward: yourself, your church, and now your community. Knowing one's congregation does not always yield the same result as knowing one's community. Changes in neighborhoods due to factors like white flight have caused white Christians to move to the suburbs. Sometimes churches move to the suburbs by selling their property to a church that looks more like the neighborhood.[15] What this means is that, especially for older congregations, there may be significant differences in the demographic makeup of the congregation and the surrounding community. This means that the preacher must not only study his congregation, but he must also be invested in his understanding of the community. This means both knowing facts and what makes the neighborhood and community unique.

I spent my first twenty-six years living in Southeastern Virginia. The region, known as Hampton Roads, has a population of more than 1.7 million but it is most known for two things: its beaches and military bases. You cannot really understand the area without understanding these two things. The United States Department of Defense has a workforce of approximately one hundred and fifty thousand with about eighty-three thousand of those being active-duty military personnel. Not surprisingly, Hampton Roads is home to the largest naval base in the world and there are churches in the area that take their role in supporting military families seriously.[16] They help spouses during deployment and they provide services to those in

15. Clint Cooper, "Chattanooga's Iconic Highland Park Baptist Church Will Move."
16. "Our Military."

uniform. Even in churches with no active-duty personnel, there is often a plan for how to make connections and serve those in the military. If a church in Hampton Roads does not have a system in place for welcoming and ministering to members of the military and their families, they do not know their community well. Their church may not have many sailors and soldiers, but they should have a structure in place to serve those in the military community.

But simply having a structure in place is not enough. Our community must know that we care for them and that can only happen after we do the work of knowing them. Manuel Ortiz warns:

> People will not want to be viewed as a "target audience," but rather as human beings with many needs who desire respect and compassion. They do not care about theological paradigms or concepts as much as they want to know that we care for them. Compassion requires solidarity, a "suffering with." Vulnerability must be mutual. It is imperative that we live in the community and participate in its life, using the same stores, schools and means of recreation. We are as enriched and as limited as they are. We begin to internalize their suffering and powerlessness.[17]

This is really the aim of knowing our community: we must love them. Knowing things like the number of homeless people in your community or the latest poverty outlook means nothing if we do not have love for those outside of our church walls. This is especially true when working with people of a different ethnicity. Richard Soulen notes, "For not until white middle class Christians come to understand the language and modes of black worship are they likely to understand either the black church or its people. And perhaps not until then will they truly understand themselves."[18]

The preacher must be a bridge-builder and that can only happen when the preacher knows the community. Stott provides the following advice:

> We need, then, to ask people questions and get them talking. We ought to know more about the Bible than they do, but they are likely to know more about the real world than we do. So we should encourage them to tell us about their home and family life, their job, their expertise and their spare-time interests. We also need to penetrate beyond their doing to their thinking. What makes them tick? How does their Christian faith motivate them? What

---

17. Ortiz, *Hispanic Challenge*, 152–53.
18. Soulen, "Black Worship and Hermeneutic."

problems do they have which impede their believing or inhibit them from applying their faith to their life? The more diverse people's backgrounds, the more we have to learn. It is important for us to listen to representatives of different generations as well as of different cultures, especially of the younger generation. The married pastor who has teenage children has no excuse not to be earthed in reality. Humble listening is indispensable to relevant preaching. It also makes preaching a co-operative enterprise as our knowledge of the Bible and other people's knowledge of the world combine to construct bridges.[19]

Knowing our community begins with the realization that Christians live as exiles in a Babylon-like world. This means that most of our neighbors do not know Christ and are in desperate need for the grace that only comes from repentance and faith. Zack Eswine observes, "Jesus preached to crowds saturated with sin, disease, and oppression. These crowds were also filled with people of varying economic, class, ethnic, and regional backgrounds. This posture makes things messy but powerful."[20] Truly knowing our community, however, is not just knowing about those who do not share the same background or history as us. It means listening to their stories and being moved by them. According to Eswine:

> A person sees a redbird on a tree limb in St. Louis, Missouri, identifies the bird as a cardinal, and keeps walking. The person assumes that once named, the bird requires no further attention, even though that person may actually know nothing about the nature, habits, and lifestyles of cardinals. Naively, we think we know what cardinals are simply because we have a name for them.
> Because we have named cultures, demographics, people groups, or philosophical movements does not mean we understand them. Moreover, the individual experience of persons within groups often challenges the tidiness of our generalized descriptions.[21]

We must know our community intimately and we do that by listening to others. Kim notes, "Listening is not a highly touted skill in our society. We reward lions that roar and not mice that squeak. Whether it's in school, society, or the church, good listeners do not receive positive reinforcement or accolades. Put differently, the art of good listening encompasses the

---

19. Stott, *Between Two Worlds*, 192.
20. Eswine, *Preaching to a Post-Everything World*, 84.
21. Eswine, *Preaching to a Post-Everything World*, 39.

peculiar knack for being uncomfortable."[22] This art of listening takes patience and purposeful management of time, especially in building margin into our schedules. Eswine explains:

> Taking time with people sometimes feels like living in an unfinished house. We tire of washing our dishes in the bathtub while we wait for the sink to be fixed. We long for convenience, routine, and certainty. But taking time with people challenges our notions of perfection. We live with the unfinished, and we are forced to remember ourselves. People need the same amount of time we were once given. They need an environment in which they can get answers wrong and find room to learn what is right.[23]

This is true to the Great Commission, where we are told to "make disciples," not just make converts. Making converts—often a one-time experience—does not require much of a Christian and while many preachers have seen their job responsibility primarily as a "soul-winner," the preacher's job is really a calling to discipleship. The gospel is shared and the ones who put their trust in Christ are then discipled, something that requires a substantial amount of time and energy from the pastor. This is a must if the preacher wants to be effective in reaching people who do not share the same history or experiences. Eswine states that preaching is mentoring. He counsels:

> When we preach, we publicly model for a community how a human being is meant by God to relate to reality. By watching the preacher, people learn how to think, act, and speak toward God, our neighbors, and the issues of our times. The preacher mentors others in what it looks like for a Christian to publicly talk from God's Word about life. For this reason, we are cautious with our cynicism, our mocking voices, and our posture to the world when we preach. Rather, we become intentional to model in our flawed way what love for God and neighbor (including enemies) looks and sounds like for a follower of Jesus.[24]

This can only come when the shepherd is actively involved in the life of both the congregation and the community at-large.

One may ask why this must be "messy," to borrow a term from Eswine. As stated throughout this work, preaching becomes messy when our audience is diverse and our preaching tears down the idols that we have

22. Kim, *Preaching with Cultural Intelligence*, 152.
23. Eswine, *Preaching to a Post-Everything World*, 15.
24. Eswine, *Preaching to a Post-Everything World*, 85.

What Preachers Can Do

allowed to be built in our churches and community. Preaching the Word faithfully each week is already a difficult task. Seeking to do that while, at the same time, working to exegete a congregation and community seems, well, messy. Gilbert observes that all of the concerns that our neighbors have, however, are addressed in our powerful gospel. He claims:

> There is no gospel "for us" that is not clothed in human culture and is not mediated through the sociocultural concerns of where we live, who we are, and what we value. Constructive pedagogy asks if our theologies of preaching are constructed with the local idioms of our students in view. In an age of suspicion hermeneutics, competing narratives, and reality redescription, without a revised understanding of what is at stake culturally and communally in contemporary preaching, our homiletical theorizing will be scantily useful.[25]

The gospel is the solution to our biggest problem but that will not get through to our neighbors unless we are able to speak in a language they understand.

One criticism that I have encountered perhaps more than any other is that this cheapens the preaching of the Word in favor of tailoring a message that makes non-Christians more comfortable. This is a valid concern, but I am not advocating for changing or cheapening the gospel message. We preach the Word with conviction and courage, but it must be done with a deep concern for the lost around us. David Hansen writes, "Market research may tell us that 40 percent of the homes in our neighborhood are run by single parents. We need to know that. But if we fail to realize that every one of those single parents is different, we cheapen their burden and their sacrifice, and we homogenize their hopes and dreams. That isn't how Jesus dealt with people."[26] We must value each person and that comes from knowing their hurts, needs, and desires.

Another criticism that I have heard is that Christian preachers should not take secular ideas and use them in their preaching. The fear, like the one previously stated, is that we will drift away from Scripture being sufficient and move closer and closer to adapting the gospel message to be more palatable to the world. Merida addresses this, writing:

> Often expositors cringe at the thought of "improving their preaching with secular communication ideas." But there are several reasons to improve your speaking skills. Paul apparently knew the

---

25. Gilbert, *Journey and Promise of African American Preaching*, 22.
26. Hansen, "Who's Listening Out There," 134.

importance of effective communication. He asked the Colossian church to pray for him that he would proclaim the mystery of Christ *clearly* (Col 4:2–4). We want to be clear, not to impress, but so that the gospel may be understood. Clarity is a moral issue, not a stylistic issue. It is an eternal issue. We should want to be clear because of what is at stake![27]

The concern for our neighbors—especially those who are people of color—is an effect of being changed by the gospel. Paul's quotations of Greek poems in Acts 17 is an example of a Christian using language understood by those outside of the church. We are agreeing with the Apostle Paul when we seek to improve our communication so that the gospel can be presented well in our preaching.

One way that we can show that we truly care about our neighbors is by speaking in a manner they can resonate with and understand. I did not have a strong southern accent, but I decided to purge a few words from my vocabulary when I moved west to Arizona. I did not want an accent or unfamiliar colloquialism to distract people from hearing the message. I wanted to sound as much like the community I served in as I could, not to be phony, but to endear myself to the people I served. Keller believes that the use of culturally accepted speech is an asset to the preacher:

> It is easy for preachers to fall either into a stiff, written style of speaking or a distractingly conversational style. Neither will be as memorable as communication marked by rhetorical devices that fit your culture. There are scores of these, and they are better picked up and "caught" (from other speakers) than "taught" and deliberately used. They include assonance, alliteration, and other kinds of parallelism. "He doesn't just talk the talk—he walks the walk." And there are a large number of less obvious but striking ways to use language memorably and movingly. However, different cultures and different generations will respond to various devices in different ways. Some will seem too florid or too highbrow or too stuffy or too manipulative.[28]

This kind of approach shows deference to the people who make up the community. With this comes the hope of every preacher: that his message will be heard and that lives will be changed for the cause of Christ.

27. Merida, *Christ-Centered Expositor*, 213.
28. Keller, *Preaching*, 178.

What Preachers Can Do

Of the four areas of study, I believe that studying one's community is the easiest because there are so many resources available. The United States Census Bureau allows one to search through all sorts of demographic data by zip code.[29] There, one can see information relating to average income, ethnic makeup of the community, and other social categories that will help the preacher know who lives around him. One of my favorite resources is from the Urban Institute.[30] They have detailed interactive maps that allow you to see data on schools, poverty, housing, and education. These tools are free and readily available to anyone with just a few clicks.

Study Your God

The last piece of advice is the most important anyone can give: study your God. This should be obvious, but I have been unpleasantly surprised at how many preachers (myself included) have lost sight of who God is. We hurry through the week with sermon preparation, home and hospital visits, and dealing with seemingly endless complaints that we rarely sit and think and study who God is and how he operates. In his book *Dangerous Calling: Confronting the Unique Challenges of Pastoral Ministry*, Paul David Tripp asserts that pastors can get so busy with ministry that they lose their passion for the work and their awe for God:

> What is the danger? It is that familiarity with the things of God will cause you to lose your awe. You've spent so much time in Scripture that its grand redemptive narrative, with its expansive wisdom, doesn't excite you anymore. You've spent so much time exegeting the atonement that you can stand at the foot of the cross with little weeping and scant rejoicing. You've spent so much time discipling others that you are no longer amazed at the reality of having been chosen to be a disciple of Jesus Christ. You've spent so much time unpacking the theology of Scripture that you've forgotten that its end game is personal holiness. You've spent so much time in strategic, local-church ministry planning that you've lost your wonder at the sovereign Planner that guides your every moment. You've spent so much time meditating on what it means to lead others in worship, but you have little private awe. It's all become so regular and normal that it fails to move you anymore; in fact, there are sad

---

29. https://www.census.gov/data.html
30. https://www.urban.org/research/data-methods/interactive-maps

moments when the wonder of grace can barely get your attention in the midst of your busy ministry schedule.[31]

Tripp argues that every preacher must be consumed by a sense of awe of God: "This means that every sermon should be prepared by a person whose study is marked by awe of God. The sermon must be delivered in awe and have as its purpose to motivate awe in those who hear."[32]

While addressing the limitations of a preacher, Carl Ellis uses the illustration of music:

> The two main components of music are tone and rhythm. These have always been part of our revelational environment. God created us to express beauty and truth musically to his glory. Song can serve as a parable of reality. We cannot, however, compose or perform music employing all the possible combinations of tone and rhythm in all possible modes of unity and diversity, form and freedom, any more than we can know all the mind of God. We are finite. Only the infinite, triune God of the Scriptures can create perfect music.[33]

Without a deep understanding of God, the preacher will often resort to his own skills and abilities. This is to his detriment as only God can "create perfect music."

I want to state this clearly: not every pastor needs advanced degrees. History has proven that many faithful and successful pastors and preachers have little to no formal education. However, theological education should not be overlooked, because it helps pastors prepare for the ministry. Whether the preacher goes to seminary or not, theological training and study is essential for success in the pulpit. I am convinced that to be a faithful expositor *and* a faithful shepherd to a congregation of diverse people, the pastor must be trained well. This certainly includes deep theological study.

The preacher who desires more theological training has a few choices. He could begin formal training in a Bible college or seminary. There is no substitute for training under established scholars who are experts in their field. For a white preacher, attending a seminary that has an ethnically diverse faculty would be most helpful. There are many preachers who, for one reason or another, cannot commit to formal education. In these cases, the preacher should seek out fellow pastors who are interested in reading

---

31. Tripp, *Dangerous Calling*, 114–15.
32. Tripp, *Dangerous Calling*, 118.
33. Ellis, Jr., *Free at Last?*, 173.

theology together. My recommendation is to find three or four pastors (preferably of a different ethnicity or cultural background) and read books together. Discuss what was written and how that applies to life as a pastor in each respective context.

Conclusion

I recognize that a work such as this has many unanswered questions. This is not a step-by-step guide on preaching, multi-ethnic ministry, or intercultural communication. Though not extensive, there are books and articles written to help the pastor preach the gospel and communicate to multi-ethnic communities more effectively. That has not been my aim through this work. Instead, my focus is to give some encouragement and assistance to the pastor who finds himself in one of two situations: either he preaches to a room full of people who look, think, and talk differently than him, or he leads a congregation that does not reflect the demographic makeup of the surrounding community. In the former case, the pastor should desire to communicate to his congregation more effectively. In the latter case, the pastor should desire to communicate to his neighbors more effectively.

My hope is that this short book will encourage pastors of already diverse churches as well as pastors who desire to 'preach without borders.' My prayer is that this introduction will bless those who have read it and spur them on to run the race that is set before us.

Bibliography

Anyabwile, Thabiti. *Reviving the Black Church: A Call to Reclaim a Sacred Institution.* Nashville: B&H, 2015.

Arthurs, Jeffrey D. *Preaching as Reminding: Stirring Memory in an Age of Forgetfulness.* Downers Grove, IL: IVP, 2017.

Atkinson, Max. *Lend Me Your Ears: All You Need to Know About Making Speeches & Presentations.* New York: Oxford University Press, 2004.

Azurdia III, Arturo G. *Spirit Empowered Preaching: Involving the Holy Spirit in Your Ministry.* Ross-shire, England: Mentor, 2010.

The Barna Group. "18-35-Year-Olds Rate the Church's Reputation for Justice." December 4, 2019. https://www.barna.com/research/churchs-reputation-for-justice/.

Blomberg, Craig. *Matthew.* Vol. 22. The New American Commentary. Nashville: Broadman & Holman, 1992.

Bock, Darrell L. *Luke: 9:51–24:53.* Vol. 2. Baker Exegetical Commentary on the New Testament. Grand Rapids, MI: Baker Academic, 1996.

Booth, Abraham. "Pastoral Cautions." In *On The Ministry: Writings And Messages From The Puritans,* edited by John Bonker, 23–49. Morrisville, NC: Lulu, 2014.

Bradley, Anthony. "Black Church, Moses and Evangelical Church." *What Is Your Salvation For?* http://www.whatisyoursalvationfor.com/blog.

Bratt, James D. *Abraham Kuyper, A Centennial Reader.* Grand Rapids, MI: Eerdmans, 1998.

Bridges, Jerry. *The Gospel for Real Life.* Colorado Springs: NavPress, 2003.

Calvin, John. *Institutes of the Christian Religion.* Accessed June 13, 2021. https://ccel.org/ccel/calvin/institutes/institutes.iii.ii.html.

Carson, D.A. *The Gospel According to John.* The Pillar New Testament Commentary. Grand Rapids, MI: Eerdmans, 1991.

Chapell, Bryan. "The Future of Expository Preaching—Parts 1 & 2." *Preaching.* https://www.preaching.com/articles/the-future-of-expository-preaching-parts-1-2/.

Bibliography

———. "The Necessity of Preaching Christ in a World Hostile to Him." In *Preaching to a Shifting Culture: 12 Perspectives on Communicating That Connects*, edited by Scott M. Gibson, 59–78. Grand Rapids, MI: Baker, 2004.

Charles, H.B., Jr. *On Preaching: Personal and Pastoral Insights for the Preparation & Practice of Preaching*. Chicago: Moody, 2015.

Cloete, David. "A False Rivalry: Gospel Preaching and Social Justice." *The Gospel Coalition*. September 8, 2020. https://africa.thegospelcoalition.org/article/false-rivalry-salvation-social-justice/.

Cooper, Clint. "Chattanooga's Iconic Highland Park Baptist Church Will Move." *Chattanooga Times Free Press*. September 10, 2012. https://www.timesfreepress.com/news/news/story/2012/sep/10/091012a01-iconic-highland-park-baptist-will-move/87458/?bcsubid=c35368d0-d18d-4271-8987-41675110d875&pbdialog=reg-wall-login-created-tfp.

Cosper, Mike. *Rhythms of Grace: How the Church's Worship Tells the Story of the Gospel*. Wheaton, IL: Crossway, 2013.

Craddock, Fred B. *Preaching*. Nashville: Abingdon, 1985.

Darling, Daniel. "Three Reasons White Pastors Need To Start Preaching on Race." May 29, 2020. https://danieldarling.com/2020/05/three-reasons-white-pastors-need-to-start-preaching-on-race/.

DeYmaz, Mark, and Harry Li. *Leading a Healthy Multi-Ethnic Church: Seven Common Challenges and How to Overcome Them*. Leadership Network Innovation. Grand Rapids, MI: Zondervan, 2010.

DeYoung, Curtiss Paul, Michael O. Emerson, George Yancey, and Karen Chai Kim. *United by Faith: The Multiracial Congregation as an Answer to the Problem of Race*. New York: Oxford University Press, 2003.

Ellis, Jr., Carl F. *Free at Last? The Gospel in the African-American Experience*. 2nd ed. Downers Grove, IL: IVP, 1996.

Elmer, Duane. *Cross-Cultural Conflict: Building Relationships for Effective Ministry*. Downers Grove, IL: IVP, 1993.

Emerson, Michael O. Foreword to *Leading a Healthy Multi-Ethnic Church: Seven Common Challenges and How to Overcome Them*. Grand Rapids, MI: Zondervan, 2010.

Emerson, Michael O., and Christian Smith. *Divided By Faith: Evangelical Religion and the Problem of Race in America*. New York: Oxford University Press, 2000.

Eswine, Zack. *Preaching to a Post-Everything World: Crafting Biblical Sermons That Connect with Our Culture*. Grand Rapids, MI: Baker, 2008.

Fea, John. "'The Town That Billy Sunday Could Not Shut down': Prohibition and Sunday's Chicago Crusade of 1918." *Illinois Historical Journal* 87. 4 (Winter 1994) 242–58.

Garland, David E. *1 Corinthians*. Baker Exegetical Commentary on the New Testament. Grand Rapids, MI: Baker Academic, 2003.

Gilbert, Greg. *What Is the Gospel?* Wheaton, IL: Crossway, 2010.

Gilbert, Kenyatta. *The Journey and Promise of African American Preaching*. Minneapolis, MN: Fortress, 2011.

Gilbreath, Edward. *Reconciliation Blues: A Black Evangelical's Inside View of White Christianity*. Downers Grove, IL: IVP, 2006.

Goldman, Ari L. "Members Elect A New Pastor At Riverside." *New York Times*. February 6, 1989, sec. B.

González, Justo L., and Pablo A. Jiménez. *Púlpito: An Introduction to Hispanic Preaching*. Nashville: Abingdon, 2005.

Bibliography

Guinness, Os. *Fool's Talk: Recovering the Art of Christian Persuasion.* Downers Grove, IL: InterVarsity, 2015.

Hampton Roads Chamber. "Our Military." https://www.hrchamber.com/page/our-military/#:~:text=The%20Hampton%20Roads%20area%20is,NATO%20command%20on%20U.S.%20soil.

Hansen, David. "Who's Listening Out There." In *Preaching to a Shifting Culture: 12 Perspectives on Communicating That Connect,* edited by Scott M. Gibson, 129–46. Grand Rapids, MI: Baker, 2004.

Helm, David. *Expositional Preaching: How We Speak God's Word Today.* Wheaton, IL: Crossway, 2014.

Hendriksen, William, and Simon J. Kistemaker. *Exposition of Galatians.* Vol. 8. New Testament Commentary. Grand Rapids, MI: Baker, 2002.

Hill, Andrew, and John H. Walton. *A Survey of the Old Testament.* Vol. 3. Grand Rapids, MI: Zondervan, 2009.

Hill, Daniel. *White Awake: An Honest Look at What It Means to Be White.* Downers Grove, IL: IVP, 2017.

Huguley, Ryan. *8 Hours or Less: Writing Faithful Sermons Faster.* Chicago: Moody, 2017.

Hyun, Dan. "Why I Preach About Racism." *Facts and Trends.* August 25, 2017. https://factsandtrends.net/2017/08/25/why-i-preach-about-racism/.

"Interview with Dr. Martin Luther King, Jr." *Meet the Press.* Washington, D.C.: National Broadcasting Company, April 17, 1960. http://okra.stanford.edu/transcription/document_images/Vol05Scans/17Apr1960_InterviewonMeetthePress.pdf.

Jensen, Phillip D., and Paul Grimmond. *The Archer and the Arrow: Preaching the Very Words of God.* Kingsford, Australia: Matthias Media, 2010.

Jones, Robert P. "Racism among White Christians Is Higher than among the Nonreligious. That's No Coincidence." *NBC News.* July 27, 2020. https://www.nbcnews.com/think/opinion/racism-among-white-christians-higher-among-nonreligious-s-no-coincidence-ncna1235045.

Keller, Timothy. *Preaching: Communicating Faith in an Age of Skepticism.* New York: Penguin, 2015.

Kim, Matthew D. *Preaching with Cultural Intelligence: Understanding the People Who Hear Our Sermons.* Grand Rapids, MI: Baker Academic, 2017.

Kistemaker, Simon J., and William Hendriksen. *Exposition of the Acts of the Apostles.* Vol. 17. New Testament Commentary. Grand Rapids, MI: Baker, 1990.

Koessler, John. *Folly, Grace, and Power: The Mysterious Act of Preaching.* Grand Rapids, MI: Zondervan, 2011.

Köstenberger, Andreas J. *John.* Baker Exegetical Commentary on the New Testament. Grand Rapids, MI: Baker Academic, 2004.

Lingenfelter, Sherwood G., and Marvin K. Mayers. *Ministering Cross-Culturally: An Incarnational Model for Personal Relationships.* 2nd ed. Grand Rapids, MI: Baker Academic, 2003.

Liu, Shuang, Zala Volcic, and Cindy Gallois. *Introducing Intercultural Communication: Global Cultures and Contexts.* London: Sage, 2012.

Livermore, David A. *Cultural Intelligence: Improving Your CQ to Engage Our Multicultural World.* Grand Rapids, MI: Baker Academic, 2009.

Lloyd-Jones, D. Martyn. *Preaching and Preachers.* 40th Anniversary Edition. Grand Rapids, MI: Zondervan, 2011.

Bibliography

Loritts, Bryan. "What Is Biblical Preaching?: Multiethnic Culture and Preaching." *Christianity Today.* December 31, 2018. https://www.christianitytoday.com/edstetzer/2018/december/what-is-biblical-preaching-multiethnic-culture-and-preachin.html.

MacArthur, John. "Social Justice and the Gospel, Part 1," August 26, 2018. https://www.gty.org/library/sermons-library/81-21/social-justice-and-the-gospel-part-1.

———. "Why Doesn't John MacArthur Add Much Application to His Sermons?" Accessed July 20, 2016. https://www.gty.org/resources/sermons/GTY117/Why-doesnt-John-MacArthur-add-much-application-to-his-sermons.

McQuoid, Stephen. *The Beginner's Guide to Expository Preaching.* Ross-shire, England: Christian Focus, 2002.

Merida, Tony. *The Christ-Centered Expositor: A Field Guide for Word-Driven Disciple Makers.* Nashville: B&H, 2016.

Mitchell, Henry H. *Black Preaching: The Recovery of a Powerful Art.* Nashville: Abingdon, 1990.

———. *The Recovery of Preaching.* New York: Harper & Row, 1977.

Moore, Russell. *Onward: Engaging the Culture Without Losing the Gospel.* Nashville: B&H, 2015.

Moss III, Otis. *Blue Note Preaching in a Post-Soul World: Finding Hope in an Age of Despair.* Louisville, KY: Westminster John Knox, 2015.

Motyer, Alec. *Preaching? Simple Teaching on Simply Preaching.* Ross-shire, England: Christian Focus, 2013.

Nichols, Tom. *The Death of Expertise: The Campaign Against Established Knowledge and Why It Matters.* New York: Oxford University Press, 2017.

Nieman, James R., and Thomas G. Rogers. *Preaching to Every Pew: Cross-Cultural Strategies.* Minneapolis: Fortress, 2001.

Orrick, Jim Scott, Brian Payne, and Ryan Fullerton. *Encountering God Through Expository Preaching: Connecting God's People to God's Presence Through God's Word.* Nashville: B&H, 2017.

Ortiz, Manuel. *The Hispanic Challenge: Opportunities Confronting the Church.* Downers Grove, IL: IVP, 1993.

Payne, J.D. *Strangers Next Door: Immigration, Migration, and Mission.* Downers Grove, IL: IVP, 2012.

Perkins, John M. *Dream With Me: Race, Love, and the Struggle We Must Win.* Grand Rapids, MI: Baker, 2017.

Platt, David. "Let Justice Roll Down Like Waters: Racism and Our Need for Repentance." Presented at the Together for the Gospel, Louisville, KY, 2018. https://t4g.org/resources/david-platt/let-justice-roll-like-waters-racism-need-repentance/.

Polhill, John B. *Acts.* Vol. 26. The New American Commentary. Nashville: Broadman & Holman, 1992.

Prince, David E. "Preaching About Race: Keeping the Big Picture in View." April 4, 2018. http://www.davidprince.com/2018/04/04/preaching-race-keeping-big-picture-view/.

Rah, Soong-Chan. *Many Colors: Cultural Intelligence for a Changing Church.* Chicago: Moody, 2010.

Rainer, Thom. "Why It Takes Five to Seven Years to Become the Pastor of a Church." *Church Answers.* August 21, 2017. https://churchanswers.com/blog/why-it-takes-five-to-seven-years-to-become-the-pastor-of-a-church/.

Bibliography

Richards, E. Randolph, and Brandon J. O'Brien. *Misreading Scripture with Western Eyes: Removing Cultural Blinders to Better Understand the Bible*. Downers Grove, IL: IVP, 2012.

Richards, John C., and Daniel Yang. "Preaching on Racism from the 'White' Pulpit: Reflections from David Platt's Talk at T4G." *The Exchange with Ed Stetzer*. April 2020. https://www.christianitytoday.com/edstetzer/2018/april/preaching-on-racism-platt.html.

Roach, Ryan. "An Acceptable Religion." Presented at the Pursuit Church, Oviedo, FL, November 15, 2015. https://pursuitorlando.com/sermons/?sermon_id=4.

Robinson, Haddon W. "The Relevance of Expository Preaching." In *Preaching to a Shifting Culture: 12 Perspectives on Communicating That Connects*, edited by Scott M. Gibson, 79–94. Grand Rapids, MI: Baker, 2004.

Sandra L. Colby and Jennifer M. Ortman. "Projections of the Size and Composition of the U.S. Population: 2014 to 2060," March 2015. http://www.census.gov/content/dam/Census/library/publications/2015/demo/p25-1143.pdf.

Schreiner, Thomas R. *Romans*. Vol. 6. Baker Exegetical Commentary on the New Testament. Grand Rapids, MI: Baker, 1998.

Schultze, Quentin J. *Communicating for Life: Christian Stewardship in Community and Media*. Grand Rapids, MI: Baker, 2000.

Senkbeil, Harold L. *The Care of Souls: Cultivating a Pastor's Heart*. Bellingham, WA: Lexham, 2019.

"Share of Population by Race/Ethnicity." *The Heller School for Social Policy and Management at Brandeis University*, 2012.

Smith, Robert, Jr. *Doctrine That Dances: Bringing Doctrinal Preaching and Teaching to Life*. Nashville: B&H, 2008.

Soulen, Richard N. "Black Worship and Hermeneutic." *The Christian Century*, February 11, 1970.

Spurgeon, Charles H. "The Wailing of Risca." *Spurgeon's Sermons: The Metropolitan Tabernacle Pulpit*, VII:22–40, 1860. http://classicchristianlibrary.com/library/spurgeon_charles/Spurgeon-Metropolitan-pt07.pdf.

Starr, Sonja B., and M. Marit Rehavi. "Racial Disparity in Federal Criminal Sentences." *Journal of Political Economy* 122.6 (2014) 1320–54.

"The Statement on Social Justice & the Gospel." https://statementonsocialjustice.com/wp-content/uploads/2018/09/SSJG-FINAL.pdf.

Stein, Robert H. *Luke*. Vol. 24. The New American Commentary. Nashville: Broadman & Holman, 1992.

Stephens, Randall J. "'Where Else Did They Copy Their Styles but from Church Groups?': Rock 'n' Roll and Pentecostalism in the 1950s South." *Church History* 85.1 (March 2016) 97–131.

Stetzer, Ed. "What Is Contextualization? Presenting the Gospel in Culturally Relevant Ways." *Christianity Today*. October 14, 2014. https://www.christianitytoday.com/edstetzer/2014/october/what-is-contextualization.html.

"Steven Furtick—Elevation "Church" Is Not For Believers." 01:50. Youtube video, 2017. https://www.youtube.com/watch?v=Lm6r6iB2QAE&ab_channel=HeIsWithUs.

Stott, John. *Between Two Worlds: The Challenge of Preaching Today*. Grand Rapids, MI: Eerdmans, 1994.

Tennent, Timothy C. "Evangelical Preaching in the Global Context." In *Preaching to a Shifting Culture: 12 Perspectives on Communicating That Connects*, edited by Scott M. Gibson, 199–214. Grand Rapids, MI: Baker, 2004.

Bibliography

Tisdale, Leonora Tubbs. *Preaching as Local Theology and Folk Art*. Minneapolis, MN: Fortress, 1997.

Tomasino, Anthony. "Diversity and Unity in Judaism before Jesus." *The Bible and Interpretation*. February 2004. https://bibleinterp.arizona.edu/articles/2004/02/tom288001.

Tripp, Paul David. *Dangerous Calling: Confronting the Unique Challenges of Pastoral Ministry*. Wheaton, IL: Crossway, 2015.

UMass Lowell. "Expert: Data Shows Many Whites Don't Connect Privilege To Race." September 22, 2020. https://www.uml.edu/News/press-releases/2020/SocialIssuesPoll092220.aspx.

Van Harn, Roger G. *Preacher, Can You Hear Us Listening?* Grand Rapids, MI: Eerdmans, 2005.

Verkuyl, Johannes. *Contemporary Missiology*. Grand Rapids, MI: Eerdmans, 1978.

Vespa, Jonathan, Lauren Medina, and David M. Manning. "Demographic Turning Points for the United States: Population Projections for 2020 to 2060." Current Population Reports. United States Census Bureau, February 2020. https://www.census.gov/content/dam/Census/library/publications/2020/demo/p25-1144.pdf.

Vines, Jerry, and Jim Shaddix. *Power in the Pulpit: How to Prepare and Delivery Expository Sermons*. Chicago: Moody, 1999.

Whack, Errin. "Choosing to Be Black Is the Epitome of White Privilege." *Politco Magazine*. June 17, 2015. https://www.politico.com/magazine/story/2015/06/black-white-privilege-rachel-dolezal-119126.

Whitlock Jr., Luder G. *Divided We Fall: Overcoming a History of Christian Disunity*. Phillipsburg, NJ: P&R, 2017.

www.ingramcontent.com/pod-product-compliance
Lightning Source LLC
Chambersburg PA
CBHW070916160426
43193CB00011B/1481